FAITH HABITS AND HOW TO FORM THEM

Emma Timms is a retreat guide, wellness coach, movement teacher and spiritual director. She runs an online community of contemplative practice called The Prayer Orchard. She is an active member in a global monastic order called the Order of the Mustard Seed. Emma, Jon and their four children live on the east coast of Scotland. She is a curious soul who comes alive in wild spaces and loves to swim in the ocean and hike in nature. She also loves a good dance at a ceilidh!

First published in Great Britain in 2025

Form
SPCK Group
Studio 101
The Record Hall
16–16A Baldwin's Gardens
London EC1N 7RJ
www.spckpublishing.co.uk

Copyright © Emma Timms 2025

The author has asserted her right under the Copyright, Designs and Patents Act, 1988, to be identified as author of this work.

All rights reserved. No part of this book may be reproduced or transmitted in any form or by any means, electronic or mechanical, including photocopying, recording, or by any information storage and retrieval system, without permission in writing from the publisher.
SPCK does not necessarily endorse the individual views contained in its publications.

The author and publisher have made every effort to ensure that the external website and email addresses included in this book are correct and up to date at the time of going to press. The author and publisher are not responsible for the content, quality or continuing accessibility of the sites.

Unless otherwise noted, Scripture quotations are taken from the New Revised Standard Version of the Bible, copyright © 1989 by the Division of Christian Education of the National Council of the Churches of Christ in the USA. Used by permission. All rights reserved.
Scripture quotations marked MSG are taken from THE MESSAGE, copyright © 1993, 2002, 2018 by Eugene H. Peterson. Used by permission of NavPress. All rights reserved. Represented by Tyndale House Publishers, Inc.
Scripture quotations marked NIV are from the HOLY BIBLE, NEW INTERNATIONAL VERSION, © 1973, 1978, 1984, International Bible Society. Used by permission of Zondervan Publishing House.

p.1: *An Altar in the World: Finding the sacred beneath our feet* copyright © 2009, B. Brown Taylor. Extract used by permission of Canterbury Press and HarperCollins US.
p.166: *The Silver Chair* by CS Lewis © copyright 1953 CS Lewis Pte Ltd.
Extract used with permission.

EU GPSR Authorised Representative
LOGOS EUROPE, 9 rue Nicolas Poussin, 17000, LA ROCHELLE, France
E-mail: Contact@logoseurope.eu

British Library Cataloguing-in-Publication Data
A catalogue record for this book is available from the British Library

ISBN 978-0-281-09131-7
eBook ISBN 978-0-281-09132-4

1 3 5 7 9 10 8 6 4 2

Typeset by Fakenham Prepress Solutions
First printed in Great Britain by Clays Ltd

eBook by Fakenham Prepress Solutions

Produced on paper from sustainable sources

FAITH HABITS AND HOW TO FORM THEM

21 seasonal practices to
strengthen your spiritual life

Emma Timms

For Jon.
I treasure our deep companionship through this wild, beautiful journey of life and faith.
Both the person I am becoming and this book simply wouldn't exist without your unending support and love.
Thank you.

Contents

Part 1
THE HISTORY

Introduction	1
My faith story	5
What is a rule of life?	13
Habit formation	16
Understanding what helps and why we struggle	16
The science of habit formation	18
This is your choice	23
Becoming a lifelong learner	24
Finding your why	25
My why – five case studies	26
What is your why?	28
Monks, saints and mystics	30
Looking back to look forward	30
Desert mothers and fathers	31
Monastic orders – ancient and modern	34
What can we learn from saints and holy people?	37
Julian of Norwich	37
St Francis of Assisi	39
St John of the Cross	40
St Teresa of Calcutta	41
St Ignatius of Loyola	42
St Catherine of Siena	43

Contents

What can we learn from monks?	45
Thomas Merton	45
Thomas Keating	46
One thing in common	47

Part 2
THE PRACTICES

How do I start?	51
What daily practices do you already do?	52
What are your current immovable commitments?	53
What is your current capacity and availability?	53
Does anything in your life need to be reduced to make space?	53
What times of day work well for you to integrate practices?	54
Are your weekends different from your weekdays?	54
Do you put personal space or others first?	54
Who can you share your plan with?	54
Daily practices	55
Lectio divina	56
Centering prayer	58
Liturgical prayer	61
Journalling	62
The examen	64
Breath prayer	68
Prayer postures	70
Intuitive movement	71
Walking	71
Swimming/running	72
Mindful movement and prayer	72
Chanting	73
Mini rituals	73

Contents

Intercession	75
Which practices are you drawn to?	76
Weekly practices	**77**
Sabbath	77
Review your week	84
Microdoses of silence, solitude and stillness	85
Prayer/talk with a soul friend	85
Church/community gathering	87
Mid-week house group/hobby/prayer group	88
Time in nature	88
Review of weekly practices	89
Monthly practices	**90**
A time of silence, solitude and stillness	91
Spiritual direction	96
Soul friend	98
The examen	98
Seasonal practices	**100**
A seasonal review	103
The four seasons	103
Inner and outer cleanses	108
The church calendar	113
Annual practices	**114**
Retreat	115
Pilgrimage	123
Mission/service of others	130
Practices for different stages of life	**133**
For parents of young children	135
For those with caring duties	139
For those with chronic illness	140
For those in a time of transition	142
For periods of intense study or heavy workload	144
For those who aren't coping and don't know why	144

Contents

Practices for your current spiritual state	**147**
Flourishing	147
Dark night of the soul	148

Part 3
THE WORKBOOK

How to pull it all together	**153**
Case study: four people's rules of life	**154**
Creating your own	**162**
Final thoughts	**165**
Acknowledgements	168
Further reading	169

Part I
THE HISTORY

Introduction

> Whoever you are, you are human. Wherever you are, you live in the world, which is just waiting for you to notice the holiness in it. So welcome to your own priesthood, practiced at the altar of your own life. The good news is that you have everything you need to begin.
> Barbara Brown Taylor[1]

I like to describe myself as an unlikely contemplative. Really unlikely, if I don't get off my phone! This is how it goes: I'll just quickly check how much caffeine is in cacao powder, because I had a headache yesterday when I didn't have it in my smoothie and maybe it was that? Ooh, this brand looks good – I've been looking for some that comes in recyclable packaging. Might as well just check Instagram, Facebook, my email, WhatsApp, the weather, the news… Look at this dog video – it's so funny the way the dog's looking at the cat!

I mean, seriously – dog videos? Am I really getting up at 5:30 a.m. to check the weather, research cacao packaging and watch dog videos? Is that how I actually want to spend my sacred, set-apart, pre-child-waking free hour? No. It isn't. Yet here I am.

None of us are immune from the time we live in. Even Paul said, 'Why is it I do what I don't want to do, and don't do what I want to?' (Romans 7:15). *Everybody* has their struggles, even the ones who look like they have it all together… or maybe especially them! It's completely normal.

We're in a time when most of us have access to the whole world via the internet. Every bit of information, temptation and

---

[1] B. Brown Taylor, *An Altar in the World: Finding the sacred beneath our feet* (Norwich: Canterbury Press, 2009), p. 17.

distraction imaginable is 'conveniently' located in our pocket. There are both new problems and old problems that go as far back as the Garden and, as I said, none of us are immune.

Last year, I was gazing over beautiful Loch Tay in the Scottish Highlands, a break that was a present for my thirty-ninth birthday. It was a cool autumn day with some low cloud on the distant mountain summits. My body felt hot and relaxed as I sunk deeply into the jacuzzi. The contrast of the chilly breeze on my face with the refreshment of my fancy spritz gave me the perfect temperature. I was deep in conversation with my husband, and we were laughing about something silly, our knees gently touching beneath the water.

It was one of those rare and perfect moments. I had everything I could desire, every need was met, every comfort attended to. But do you know what I found myself talking about?

'We could come back here next year for my fortieth birthday.'

'Wouldn't this be fun in a group?'

'You know my mum would enjoy this too; maybe I should find a time to come along with her.'

Future plans occupied my mind and started spilling out of my mouth. My every need was met, my body had every sensation it could want to be fully present and soak in the moment, but my mind had raced ahead and I was no longer completely there.

I'm not sure if you relate to this sense of being pulled back or forward in your mind, but being pulled forward is very normal for me. I'm a Seven on the Enneagram ('the Enthusiast'),[2] which means that, left unchecked, I can be all about the next thing, trying to keep my life moving and pushing forward at all times.

---

[2] 'The Enneagram: An Introduction', The Center for Action and Contemplation, 24 April 2016: https://cac.org/daily-meditations/the-enneagram-an-introduction/ (accessed 20 January 2025).

The Enneagram gained popularity as a tool within spiritual direction. Today it is widely taught as a way of understanding personality, addiction, relationships and vocation.

The fact that I noticed this happening, however, was less normal for me. I was able to catch myself in the familiar pattern of behaviour, name it, release it and return to the present – back to feeling that warmth on my skin and delighting in the view and the company.

I have been bumbling my way along this contemplative path for the past eight years. But I had been searching for it over the seven years prior to that as well, since I had my second child. I had only been a Christian for five years before becoming a mother. My 'spiritual life' consisted of going to church, going to prayer meetings, serving in the church and reading my Bible. Well, when I had a baby and a toddler, nearly all of those became unavailable to me overnight. I spent most of the service in the crèche, and I either couldn't make prayer meetings or couldn't concentrate or participate fully when I was there. I wasn't available to serve in the church the way I used to, and I was too tired to read my Bible, let alone study it. So what was I supposed to do? I knew theoretically that God was always present, but I no longer knew how to access that presence. I knew theoretically that my value and worth didn't come from what I did, but I sure did struggle to let go and find a sense of identity in this new season of life.

So I started searching.

And it wasn't easy.

Yet slowly but surely, I found new ways both to be with God and to live out my faith. It's hard to summarise accurately the journey I went on, but I suppose it went something like this:

I can't attend the Sunday service very often, so can I find God by loving and speaking to the mum who seems lonely in the crèche? I can't manage the prayer meetings, so can I learn to pray as I go and pray alone when I can? I can't serve in my old ways, God, so can you show me new ways to love others in my new reality? I'm too tired to study my Bible, so can I carry a tiny fragment of Scripture around in my heart through the day? I'm struggling to 'see' God in ways

I used to, so can I look for the Divine in my baby's smile or find a reflection of God in the blossoming tree I'm passing? This spiritual journey of discovery went on and I documented each step from that day fifteen years ago to the present. This book is the result of fifteen years of writing and wrestling. When I started it, I thought it would take me two! It was a good job I didn't know back then the process and the journey the Spirit would lead me on, or I never would have started. It turns out that my idea of timing and transformation is on a slightly different timescale from God's.

The other pivotal part of my journey was a geographical move eight years ago. This became the catalyst for a bigger expansion of faith. I wrestled with the theology and culture of the faith I was formed in until, at the peak of my struggle, my hair quite literally began to fall out. I found the process of moving away from some entrenched beliefs extremely painful, isolating and disorientating. Some might call that a deconstruction, but I like to think of it more as a wilderness season of life that led to a deepening and expanding of my faith.

I have since had time to 're-construct' and re-imagine my faith, to let go and release those things I no longer align with, while at the same time being able to include and enjoy all the good things and gifts from the faith tradition of my youth: to allow what I learned in my formative faith years to exist together alongside the wonderful rich contemplative Christianity I find myself a part of now. It's my belief that each part of the Church has a gift to bring and something to teach us. I love that I've come to a place now where I'm more concerned with listening and learning than with who's right or wrong.

Sometimes I look at the stars or ponder the way the moon controls the tides and I feel like an ant trying to grasp quantum physics, as I attempt to understand the vastness and wonder of God. Frankly, I imagine we've all got it a bit wrong, and I'm happy, in fact I'm relieved, to choose faith and mystery over exact doctrine and certainty.

My faith story

I would love to take a moment to go back to the very beginning of my faith and share it with you. My story and the bits I've learned along the way are all I really have to offer and all that I know for sure is absolutely true.

When I was nineteen years old, I dropped out of my first degree and went to Newquay in Cornwall to spend the summer working and having fun. I lived in a shed; no, that's not a typo... It was a shed that I shared with three other young women outside a local backpackers' hostel. The hostels were all far too busy in the summer with guests paying the nightly rate, so if you wanted to stay on workers' wages, it was into the outbuildings you went!

When I wasn't working or surfing, I was partying. Hard. One morning after a spectacularly colourful night, I had wandered away from the crowd of backpackers and was sitting alone on a clifftop. For context, let's just say I hadn't been making the world's most intelligent choices, and I was feeling pretty lost and rubbish about myself. I looked out over the roaring Atlantic Ocean, at the sky with the sun beaming through the clouds like the cover of the hymn book we used to sing from in primary school. As I gazed out in my hungover stupor, I didn't audibly hear, but, rather, I felt a voice from within saying very clearly the words, 'What you do isn't who you are.' Those were the exact words my heart needed to hear that day.

I don't know how else to explain the experience, except that I knew it was God. That very first encounter I had was what you might call a mystical one. No one led me to God; the encounter came from within. So I immediately called the only Christian I knew – the mum of my friend from school (thank you, Jane!). Long story short, the following week I made my way to church via the advice of a couple of Christians also living the 'Newquay lifestyle' whom I had met in the hostel. They weren't going to the church themselves, but they encouraged me to go and told me how to get there.

I walked in nervous and alone and was greeted with a massive hug from a very smiley stranger. It was a full-blown charismatic Pentecostal meeting with flags and everything! It's important to note here that the only church I had ever been into was a cathedral with my school at Christmas. Let's just say it was quite different from that. I sat there bewildered through the whole thing and pretty ready to leave. At the end, the pastor said he felt he had quite a specific 'word from God' for someone. What happened next sounds like fiction, but I promise you it is entirely true. Before the pastor even spoke, I knew that out of the 200 people in the room, that 'word' was going to be for me. I'm not sure how important that fact is. I once bought a lottery ticket and was quite sure I would win, which shows I can be a self-oriented type of person. That aside, my heart began to pound, my mouth went dry, and I just stared at him from the back where I was seated.

He said, 'I feel like God wants to tell someone, "What you do isn't who you are."'

Those same words that I'd felt within my own heart a week earlier and told no one about were now coming out of this stranger's mouth!

He said, 'If that's relevant to someone here, please come to the front.'

I pondered the statistical impossibility that I could think something in my own head and then this guy could know it, and decided to stand up. In my white-and-orange spotted summer dress, I pushed my way along from the middle of an overcrowded row and marched straight up to him – and he prayed for me to 'receive Jesus'. Even though I didn't really know what that meant, I agreed with the prayer and went along with it. I learned afterwards what I'd just signed up for! I think it's fair to say that it was a miracle.

I was firmly rooted in the Pentecostal denomination of Christianity from the age of nineteen to thirty-three. It was a wonderful launchpad into my path of faith and I am for ever grateful to that church and tradition. I still benefit from some of those early teachings and encounters today. They taught me to expect the presence and action of God in my life, and that complements the contemplative path I am now on well.

I've always been a full-of-life, curious kind of person. With no faith as part of my upbringing, I had *a lot* of questions, and the church *always* had the answers! If I questioned these answers or they didn't feel right, I was seldom offered other perspectives from different parts of the Christian tradition. Everything always had quite a straightforward answer. I was taught that:

'Some things are beyond our understanding.'

'This is what the Bible says, so we have to believe it.'

'The word of God is absolute truth.'

'His ways are not our ways.'

I'm not here to argue with any of those statements, but the way they were presented was difficult, and there was very little room for interpretation and nuance. For example, two people can believe the word of God is absolute truth but each mean something different when they say it. Just ask a Baptist, a Pentecostal, a Greek Orthodox, a High Anglican and a Catholic the same question and see the variety of answers you get. Who's right?

I was nineteen when I asked questions, and I had no faith background, so I did as I was told – not really because I'm a rule-follower per se, but more because my drive for security and survival was high, and, as everybody knows, you're always safest firmly in the pack.

I continued to establish myself in that church, and after eighteen months I was part of the furniture. My natural gift of communication was noticed and given a chance to flourish. I've always been good at adapting to what is expected of me; you might say I'm a quick learner. So, there I was; my questions were repressed, but I was happily tootling along with my new-found faith family and with the destructive behaviours of my teenage years firmly behind me. I felt good. I had also left a string of short-lived, unhelpful relationships and was enjoying single life.

Then suddenly into this story walked my future husband. Jon was the brother of the youth pastor, someone who had grown up in a Christian home and had walked away from his faith as a teenager. The short story is that we met and fell in love. With as much passion as I walked into my life of faith, I walked back out of it.

In one particular moment of high drama, I remember ceremoniously walking into the church bookshop, slamming all my Christian books on the counter, declaring I wouldn't be needing them anymore and marching out. I left a lot of kind people – who had loved me well – confused and heartbroken. Jon moved in just six weeks after our first date, which was difficult for the church. One well-meaning lady wrote me a letter saying that I was like the crowd spitting on Jesus' face on his way to the cross.

It was a tough time, but once I make my mind up, I'm a hard ship to turn. Jon was my first experience of real love and I just couldn't let him go. I also couldn't exist in the tension it created. I'm sure you get the sense already that I'm an 'all-in' kind of person. The black-and-white teaching I was living under at that time just compounded my natural tendencies, leaving me nowhere to go. It was Jon or God. I chose Jon, the love I could tangibly hold.

A little over a year later, I had another dramatic encounter with God via a stranger on a train. She spoke miraculously and directly into my life, and I knew I could no longer turn my back on my faith. I was so happy and in love, but I missed God.

I had a problem, though; Jon and I were going travelling in six weeks' time and planned to get married on our return eighteen months later. It was all booked. I was back in that tension I had so skilfully avoided.

I know now that Jon had been quietly and fearfully waiting for that day to come – the day that I announced I wanted to go back to my faith. And here it was. My heart was pounding as we sat down together for dinner that night. I told him about my encounter on the train and said that I loved him so much, but I couldn't keep running away from God. As these words came tumbling out of my mouth, I was certain that, by saying yes to God and what I believed this required of me, I was saying no to Jon and that he would walk away.

He listened silently, his body slowly tensing. Jon is a Nine on the Enneagram, so one of his biggest drivers is to have peace, and here I was presenting to him the biggest disrupter of peace for his world. He said pretty much nothing as I became more and more hysterical, telling the only man I have ever loved that I couldn't see a way forward. He quietly got up from the table and said he was going for a walk.

I was left absolutely devastated, with everything I had planned and hoped for, my future, quite literally walking out the door. He came back some time later and said that although he couldn't promise he would ever have a faith, he also couldn't lose me. He said he would open his heart to the possibility that God was real and see what happened, and, to reduce the tension I was feeling, that we should move our wedding forward to before we went travelling. And that's what we did.

In just six weeks I finished my degree, sold the house and planned a wedding, and we managed to get married the day before we hit the road. My church wouldn't marry us because Jon wasn't a believer. I felt peaceful about proceeding instead at the local Church of England church and we were married on a hot, sunny June day. The very next morning, we left to travel the world for a year.

Three days into our very long honeymoon, Jon experienced a miraculous healing and encounter with God. He was on a toilet in Bangkok! It's a great story, but not mine to tell. If you meet him, you should definitely ask him about it, though! In the years since, he has gone from someone who couldn't stand church to leading one... the humour of God's invitations never ceases to amaze me!

They always say life makes sense when you look backwards, and I can see now that God was preparing us both from the very beginning for the path we are on now. We spent that first year of marriage finding God in nature, each other, the occasional church and one bootleg Switchfoot CD from Khao San Road. God was inviting us to broaden our horizons right from the beginning. Some important seeds were deeply buried in that time, and it would be another decade before we saw them push through the soil.

We finished travelling, and I came home pregnant with the first of our four children. A lot of what we had learned about the vastness of God lay dormant as we started a family and fell into the rhythms of church. We went back to worship at the church where I came to faith. We both had our struggles, but we stayed for ten years until the spiritual claustrophobia built to explosion point and we left Cornwall, travelling 600 miles north to Scotland to plant a creative expression of Church. We began to explore building an expansive community embedded in contemplative values and practices, and eventually found family in the ecumenically diverse and inclusive 24-7 Prayer community.

When I discovered contemplative Christianity shortly after moving, I came home spiritually. I finally found what I had been searching for all those years ago as a young and bewildered mother.

I began to learn and implement practices that really transformed me. I began not just to know about God, but to experience the living presence of the Trinity both within me and around me. I began not just to change my behaviours, but to deal with their root causes. I began to see my difficulties not so much as something to feel shame about, but as my place of need, where I was met with compassion and encountered the limitless, transformative love of God.

I began to uncover the depths of who I really am. Practices such as the examen, centering prayer and solitude are slowly but surely freeing me from all that grip and distort. I am continually met by grace and love in the places of my deepest need and brokenness.

Rhythms such as Sabbath and seeing a spiritual director ground me and sustain me in indescribable ways. Living alongside the natural and church seasons gives me both flow and stability.

All this backstory serves to show that my faith hasn't expanded easily. My circumstances as a working mum of four aren't the easiest for cultivating practices of silence, solitude and stillness. I don't have the natural personality that would predispose me to a life of discipline. Yet here I am, the least likely contemplative you will ever meet!

Fast forward to the present moment: it is autumn at Loch Tay again, and we did in fact return to the jacuzzi for my fortieth birthday. One year on and this time I observed. I didn't have a mind that was skipping ahead to future plans, but a mind that was fully present to the joy of the moment. I leaned back, sipped my fancy spritz and smiled.

Does this neat bookend to my story mean I've arrived? Of course not. I can and will share with you throughout this book the endless stories of my struggles. I do this to show that there is fruit to contemplative practice and that it does transform you. I hope it gives you hope.

Let's begin a journey together, exploring what a year of spiritual practice could look like for *you*. How can we live out our days, weeks, months and seasons to encounter God's living presence amid the busyness and unpredictability of life in the real world?

How does an ordinary person – the stay-at-home parent, the businessperson, the minister or the person whose faith or health is falling apart – abide in the vine, float in the river, practise the presence, join the divine dance?

How can we craft rhythms and practices that are firm enough to support us, but flexible enough to accommodate reality? It's all well and good having a prayer rhythm, but what about when you wake up and the cat has vomited all over the carpet, or you have a migraine? How can we look up from our devices for long enough to notice what's around us and begin the process of change?

I think the key to this can be found as far back as the fourth century AD, in differing expressions throughout Christian history. This key is 'a rule of life'.

What is a rule of life?

> A rule of life offers unique and regular rhythms that free and open each person to the will and presence of Christ. The spiritual practices of a rule provide a way to partner with the Holy Spirit for personal transformation.
> Adele Ahlberg Calhoun[3]

Simply put, a person's 'rule of life' is made up of the rhythms and practices they commit to. These help them intentionally live in alignment with their values and deepen their life in God. We'll dig deeper into these practices to help you find the combination that makes up your rule of life, and there will be plenty of examples along the way to help you put it into practice.

Back when my kids were really small and all my normal practices went out the window, I was searching for something that turned out to be a rule of life. It was a way I could stay connected to God, be transformed and feel alive in my purpose and my personhood. I had no language or tools for it back then, and it would be many years before I even heard the term, but I was led through the wilderness, riding on the back of my own desire and determination. God helped me to build a rule of life with what was in my hands, which wasn't much!

As I mentioned, there is a saying that life makes sense when you look backwards. I can also see now what a miracle it was. I was a young, overwhelmed, exhausted mother. All I had going for me was my drive and willingness to search, and the humility to ask questions and learn from anyone who had a scrap of anything for

---
3 A. Ahlberg Calhoun, *Spiritual Disciplines Handbook: Practices That Transform Us*, revised and expanded ed. (Downers Grove, IL: IVP Books, 2015), p. 37.

me. In my spiritual barrenness, the ground of God's Spirit was fertile and rich. Even though I wasn't aware at the time, I can see now that I was led. It was hard, but eventually I did get to that tiny oasis in the desert. Fifteen years on, it has palm trees and everything, and it's big enough for others to come and be refreshed. Part of that refreshment is the online contemplative prayer community I've built called The Prayer Orchard, part of it is the work I do leading my local Christian community, and part of it you are holding in your hands right now.

How about you?

I can't think of any person of faith who wouldn't benefit from a rule of life. You may find that, without realising it, you already have one, but maybe you just don't call it that. If you are part of a church or community, eat meals, get up and go to bed at a time of your choosing, or if you regularly pray alone or with others or read your Bible, then you have a rule. You have habits. All of us have a way we live, whether it is conscious or not.

Rules of life first arose among the desert mothers and fathers and then in organised monasteries and convents, which we will explore more in the next chapter. Now they are used by modern lay monastic orders and have thereby come into the hands of ordinary people. It makes me think of the journey the Bible has taken. It used to be read only by priests, then only by people who read Latin, and then eventually by everyone.

Certainly, the very fixed and prescriptive rules of life, such as the Rule of St Benedict, are best suited to monasteries. You can't just not feed your baby because you're down in vigils, or not go to the Monday morning office meeting because you're at confession – it's not realistic!

However, we can take the essence and heart of a rule and build our own flexible and adaptable one – that's suitable for ordinary people such as you and me; people from all walks of life who are interested in spiritual formation and living a transformative life more deeply connected to God.

I think the best analogy I have heard is that a rule of life is like a trellis. You know, one of those wooden or wire structures that people have on a wall of their house or in a greenhouse, with flowers or vegetables guided to grow up it. It is a support system that helps your life to grow and flourish. The rule of life is the trellis, and your life is the flower. The rule helps your life to not fall down and guides your direction. It stops it from being destroyed by a storm and literally provides something for you to cling on to.

It is not your life. It is not the point of your life. You can definitely live without one. But it will help you to cultivate the life Jesus invites us into, especially if you want to live a life that overflows from connection to God. One of the reasons it helps, and one of the reasons why organisations such as monasteries function so well, is because of how we as humans form habits. Whether we like it or not, there are certain patterns to this, and understanding them is so helpful.

Habit formation

We all have different personalities, of course. Some of us thrive on routine and some of us do better with lots of variety. But the science behind habit formation remains the same, whether we perceive habits as 'good' or 'bad'. The mere exposure effect or familiarity principle teaches us that we feel safe and comforted by what we know, even if our habits don't do us any good. This is part of our survival mechanism: back in the day, familiar meant safe and change could mean danger.

Understanding what helps and why we struggle

As explained by Pilat and Krastev, 'The mere exposure effect describes our tendency to develop preferences for things simply because we are familiar with them. For this reason, it is also known as the familiarity principle.'[4]

Smartphones are a great example of this theory in action because they are such a widespread addiction, and boy, don't the people who make those pretty little apps and notifications just know it? Cheap dopamine hit, anyone?

The following example is how it plays out. Let's just say you have a habit of waking up and checking your phone. This happens every day. Maybe you feel it drains your energy a bit but you continue to do the same thing.

Then you go on holiday for a couple of weeks and don't take your phone, so in the morning you wake up and just sit for a minute,

---
4 D. Pilat and S. Krastev, 'Why do we prefer things that we are familiar with? The Mere Exposure Effect, explained', The Decision Lab: https://thedecisionlab.com/biases/mere-exposure-effect (accessed 20 January 2025).

maybe reading a little. At first, it feels uncomfortable because your body has got used to the stimulation, and even the drained feeling afterwards has become familiar. Remember the familiarity principle – your nervous system perceives familiar as safe.

But after a few days on holiday, you notice you feel so much better, so when you get back home, you think: 'I'm not going to check my phone in the morning anymore. It makes me feel rubbish.'

For a few days, you manage this by willpower alone. Then one morning you genuinely need to have it by your bed and check it because a family member is unwell. On waking you look for any messages or missed calls from that family member. While you're there, you just quickly check your social media and your work email, and that familiar habit feels good. In fact, after a break from it, it feels really good. 'Ding ding ding' goes the dopamine in your brain. No harm done, you tell yourself, it's just one day.

The next day you have a quick look because there is that important thing going on at work, and it doesn't matter because it's only once – that is the addiction, an actual chemical process in your brain, drawing you in; it isn't because you're weak – and before you know it, you slip back into your old habit of checking your phone again every morning... It's so frustrating! Now you're doing it and you're feeling bad and you can't stop, and you're absolutely sick of this cycle! Sound familiar?

Maybe the phone thing actually isn't a problem for you, and that's great. But this applies to any habit, and unless you are actually Jesus, I promise you, you've got something. Speaking personally, I know I have multiple somethings! In fact, I can't even pull the Jesus card on this... Do the temptations in the desert ring any bells (Matthew 4:1–11)? Even Jesus had to wrestle with the temptations of power, security and affection. He showed us the way to follow him into freedom, but more on that later.

So what is a good example for you? A glass of wine after a hard day, biscuits when you're bored, porn or unhealthy fantasising, working late to avoid difficult things at home? It's anything we turn to for comfort, where we avoid our real feelings and choose a sense of relief over a true restoration. And it isn't because we are weak, it's because our bodies want to survive – and we are addicted. We are going to have to tap into the science a bit more now so that you can see how habits become so ingrained, and why the freedom that Christ invites us into is so wonderful.

The science of habit formation

The science that lies behind this is amazing and has always been known but can now be proven. It totally reframes what a lot of us have been taught in the Church about addiction, bad habits and our struggles. Our sin, you may be used to calling it.

Our nervous system and our mammalian/instinctive brain have two goals: to further the human race and to keep us alive. They have no idea or interest in nuances and social etiquette, or in keeping our neighbours or church community happy. Our nervous system wants us to survive. Now, I know that's not very pretty or churchy, but it is true. Don't get me wrong, we do have our prefrontal cortex and with it the ability to make good choices and so on, which means we aren't the same as other animals. But when we are frightened, in danger, addicted or misunderstood, without intervention, the instinctive part of our brain kicks in and can drive our choices!

The other fascinating thing is that the nervous system initially has no idea of the difference between real or perceived threat – it just wants to protect you, no matter the cost. This is our primitive brain, which has remained the same even though other parts of us have developed and evolved. It also has no idea of modern advancements in medicine or anything like that; again, it will just work to help you survive. This is why after an injury, your body will brace and tighten. This may be unhelpful now, but in the old days, if you fell over and broke a bone in your back running from a tiger, that bracing would give you the best chance of survival, before A&E and bone-setting existed. Actually, a random but incredible fact while we are on the subject: do you know what scientists say is the first sign of a civilised society? It's not toolmaking or speech – it's the correct healing of a broken femur bone, because that means someone else stayed back and helped that person to get food and survive. We've come a long way!

Another fascinating thing about the nervous system is that it has no idea of what you're actually stressed about when you get all stressed over too many emails or your kids fighting. It just assumes stress is a threat. So, if you don't actively pause and engage your higher brain – which, by the way, a regular practice of contemplative prayer helps you learn to do – it assumes the presence of the things our ancestors dealt with, such as an impending food shortage or being approached by a grizzly bear. It doesn't know that it's a passive aggressive comment from Uncle Steve at Christmas, or being late for work on the one day your boss has decided to visit your department. It has no clue – it just goes into survival mode, shuts down your digestion, starts storing fat from everything you eat in case it's a famine, tenses your muscles and keeps you awake at night pumping cortisol so you can make a run for it if you need to. Your nervous system is really trying to help you. We need tools to tell it it's OK and help it to regulate.

The important takeaway here is that there are more reasons for your struggles than lack of willpower. There are more reasons why leaving old destructive ways behind can be hard. It is definitely *not* because we are bad people or 'sinners'. It's because there are needs in our lives that either didn't get met, or we perceived that they didn't, when we were very young. Young here often means before conscious memory: under five years old. And they can drive our behaviour as adults.

It is true that we all need transformation. That is the journey we are invited on when we follow the incredible example of love in the life of Christ.

Fr Thomas Keating did some astounding work on these underlying needs, which he named 'programs for happiness'. He divided them into three categories of things that we need as humans: things that we go looking for. These are power and control, security and survival, and affection and esteem. They are all healthy things when they are in balance: things that we get in deep union with God and others. But they are all things we don't tend to get enough of in an imperfect world. They align with Jesus' temptations in the desert that I mentioned earlier. Bread into stones – security and survival. Jumping off the Temple – affection and esteem. Power over the nations – power and control. I highly recommend Fr Thomas's work on this; it's a book in itself.

Back to the habit we can't break – checking our phone in the morning. What do we do? Are we doomed to be driven by our primitive brains and program for happiness for ever? Absolutely not.

The transformation that Christ invites us into is available and backed up by modern brain science. We *can* form new habits; this has been proven over the past twenty years. We know now that the brain has neuroplasticity, which basically means it's designed for renewal and transformation. We can change the wiring in our brains for good. In her book *Practice the Pause*, Caroline Oakes goes into this brain science extensively. She says, 'It is the call to begin the journey of responding less from our reactive and fearful early, primal brain and respond more from our more human, higher-level thinking and loving brain.'[5]

We can ask why we are turning to these things for relief. We can turn towards God and genuine connection with others, towards

---

[5] C. Oakes, *Practice the Pause: Jesus' Contemplative Practice, New Brain Science, and What It Means to Be Fully Human* (Minneapolis, MN: Broadleaf Books, 2023), p. 24.

those unmet places in ourselves with love and compassion, and begin to heal. Jesus is the healer of our souls, and often a therapist can be invaluable too, as you can't always just pray this stuff away. Certainly, you can very rarely fix anything through just renouncing and ignoring and shame. Brené Brown has done some groundbreaking work on the power of shame and how it keeps us trapped. We can't change these scared, unloved, broken places in ourselves through hating them, ignoring them and shaming them. The Church hasn't always done a good job here, unfortunately. Lots of us are more than aware of what we are struggling with and what we shouldn't be doing, but we feel powerless to stop. We feel ashamed, and bad teaching and theology about sin really don't help. We need the tools to help us transform, and here they are!

Let's walk through a way of kicking this phone habit – as an example – together. First of all, decide that you are no longer going to feel bad, surprised or ashamed that this is a difficult habit to kick. It's designed to be addictive! It is literally built by experts to reward your brain and get you addicted to the little feeling of pleasure and satisfaction that comes when you see a notification or when you scroll. It's even designed for you to feel comforted by the slightly numb feeling you get after. OK, no more guilt: honestly, it's hard to hear, but our stuff reduces us to lambs being led to slaughter.

Then you can choose to decide that fine, this is hard and it's not my fault, but I don't want to do it anymore. The Alcoholics Anonymous Twelve-Steps programme works because it follows the science of our brains and bodies.

Once you have accepted you have a problem and that you want to change it, you need a plan. You want to be kind and make this as easy as possible, working *with* rather than against yourself. So stop using the excuse, 'Oh, it's my alarm so I need it by my bed'; just go out and buy an alarm clock. Then choose to leave the phone downstairs. Obviously, there are always exceptions – you may be a nurse on call, your teenager may be out partying – but this is generally realistic for most of us. This initial plan helps to remove the temptation. We then accept and anticipate that when we wake up for the first few days or even weeks, we are going to want to reach for our phone and we are going to miss it. That's OK – don't feel bad. You're used to it; your body wants the dopamine and the comfort. Have something else ready instead, maybe a journal or a daily practice that you've identified and that you would like to have in your rule of life. You can now spend on this the amount of time you would normally spend scrolling. It takes about sixty-six repetitions to build a new habit, because this stuff really gets under our skin. So for about two months, you are going to need to have really good boundaries, and maybe some support/accountability from a good friend with whom you can check in.

Your nervous system will have become used to not getting the dopamine hits and it will perceive your new habit – the one you actually want in your life, such as the journalling, prayer or reading – as safe.

You can replace this morning phone addiction problem of mine with anything, as I said. The biscuits when you're bored can slowly become a walk seeing the beauty of God in the way the trees move; the fantasy on the way home from the gym can become the prayer for your friends and family.

If you are reading this and you're battling an addiction, then it is important that you seek professional help and support from medical professionals, therapists, support groups, charities, churches and hopefully a combination of many of these. But also please know that shame has no place here. God doesn't make you feel shame and shame won't serve you as you tackle this. Digging a little deeper and beneath the addiction, you will find a little boy or girl who either didn't get their needs met or perceived that they didn't and are just trying to meet them. That little boy or girl in you needs your love, not your judgement. They need love from you, from the Church and from God.

In my wellness coaching work, I see so many people who know the kinds of lives they want to live and are frustrated that they can't break the unhelpful patterns or stick to the new, healthier habits that will help them get to where they want to be. The last thing on earth I would want is for someone to pick up this book, feel full of hope and excitement, build a rule of life, follow it for, say, three weeks, and then see it fall apart and give up. Another failed attempt at transformation… it's just soul-destroying.

However, if science can help us learn about bad habits, then we can use it to form good ones, and to help us build and sustain a rule of life. It can help us avoid pitfalls and show us what to do when we inevitably fall off track. We can understand it takes time to build new habits, and we are going to have to foster some discipline. Consistency is comforting to the nervous system, so we are going to need some commitment to daily habits… just like the monks of old.

This is your choice

It's powerful and important that you know that. Your strong intention to do this points your energy in the direction you want it to go, towards God. Because, after fifteen years of trying, failing and trying again, I can tell you that this is not going to be plain sailing. Those 'programs for happiness' that we just learned about are going to scream and stamp their feet. Your ego is not going to go down without a fight for ever. Choosing a path of humility, forgiveness, appropriate self-sacrifice and love is going to bring about some inner wrestling as we edge our way more and more towards freedom.

Becoming a lifelong learner

Transformation takes time. We will be going from glory to glory until we die. In case no one has told you, we never arrive. I won't, you won't, the leaders you know won't, the archbishop won't, Paul never did, Mother Teresa didn't and neither did St John of the Cross. In fact, the closer people get to the heart of God, the more aware of their need they become. We might as well face that before we start. We are always going to have to come at life with the posture of a learner.

One of the best attitudes I have tried to adopt, which I have learned from the monastic order I am part of, is to keep learning central. I am *always* going to need to learn. To keep a soft open heart, while at the same time keeping in constant view the things about my faith that hold me like an anchor. That is the tension: to be firm enough to be able to stand for and be held by something without becoming superior and hard-hearted, and to be tender, humble and open-hearted enough to truly maintain the posture of a learner. If you aren't sure how to start, look at Jesus.

It is about approaching each day as a beginner, coming to it afresh humbly, ready and willing to listen. It fosters a living faith, rather than religion. It resists pride and the ego, the biggest stumbling blocks to a life of faith. It's going to help you live a transformed life, to help you grow into one of those really kind elderly people who are never in a rush and still have a glint in their eye. I hope I get to be a wonderful elderly person like that! Again, this is your choice.

Finding your why

> Whoever hammers a lump of iron first decides what he is going to make of it, a scythe, a sword, or an axe. Even so we ought to make up our minds what kind of virtue we want to forge or we labour in vain.
> Abba Anthony, desert father[6]

The final thing I want to talk about before we explore the history behind rules of life is 'finding your why'. This is essential.

You need to know why you are actually doing this. Why do you want to go through the hard work of transformation? Why do you want to live by a rule and develop habits and commitments, when no one is making you? In the monastic order I am part of, the Order of the Mustard Seed, we take vows. There's a season of preparation for about a year to make sure we want to take these vows. We live by the three core values and work them out through six practices. When monks and nuns make their life-changing vows, they often have a longer time of preparation. Franciscan friars, for example, spend three to six years making temporary vows before they take final vows. Maybe you could set aside some time as you work through this chapter and really think about *why* you want to create a rule of life.

This will provide both a map and an anchor, so when you consider a practice you already do, or want to implement a new one, you can look back and see if it is in alignment with your 'why'. We want what we do to point us firmly in the direction of where we want to go, or, more importantly, who we want to become.

---

[6] M. B. Pennington, *The Living Testament: The Essential Writings of Christianity Since the Bible* (HarperCollins, 1985), p. 66.

I asked several friends who live by a rule of life to condense their 'why' into five sentences as an example. Just like the lives of the monks, saints and mystics that we'll explore in the next chapter, these people's devotion, commitment and love of God are evident. But the way they each worked their 'why' varied greatly because they were different people in different circumstances, with different drivers. I want you to see what some of that diversity looks like today.

My why – five case studies

Me

1 I want to love my family well.
2 If I'm choosing to believe God is real, that I can walk with, know and be known by the creator of this incredible world, then I want to experience as much of that relationship as possible.
3 I want to live on purpose. I don't want life to just happen to me. I want to live awake, making conscious choices, not on autopilot.
4 I don't want to be driven by my false self/ego/programs for happiness. I want to know the true me and I want that self, in union with the heart of God, to drive my life.
5 I want to have the capacity to provide shelter from the storms of life for others; to become a safe space for people to heal and grow.

Debbie Garrick – development officer

1 I'm easily distracted. My rule of life helps me focus on what is most important: my relationship with Jesus.
2 As a single adult, accountability can sometimes be challenging. Having a rule of life provides a framework that keeps me loyal

to the vows I have taken to be true, to be kind and to share Christ with others.
3 I view a rule of life as the ultimate 'maker space', where God is free to shape and mould me. It is the space where he is constantly making all things new.
4 I think of my rule of life as – to use the traditional term – 'customary', because I want his habits to be my habits.
5 A rule of life is a haven. It is discipline in the midst of chaos, and peace away from the noise of the world.

Jill Weber – global convener of the Order of the Mustard Seed

1 I want to find ways to open myself more to God so that he can do the things in me that I cannot do for myself.
2 I want my life to be characterised by the presence, personality and power of God.
3 I want to pray, serve and love.
4 I want to become love.
5 I want to live an abundant, fruitful life.

Jon Timms – church leader and charity worker

1 To cultivate deep union with God. My whole being is made for this. A rhythm of life creates and holds a habitat for the soul to be nourished.
2 Rhythms ensure balance. As a type Nine on the Enneagram, harmony and balance are central to my own sense of well-being.
3 A rule of life realigns me to Jesus' way, his invitations and his pace, especially when I drift and go astray.
4 It reminds me and reorients me to the gifts that bring life and joy – namely God, family, prayer-filled peace, beauty, creativity and community.
5 I'm simply a better human when I follow a rhythm/rule of

life – free to love my wife, family, friends, neighbours and community with depth and authenticity.

Vicky Allen – writer, artist and charity worker

1. To live a life of deepening union with God – exploring the wonder and delight of divine mystery.
2. To be attentive to how my faith shifts and moves over time, and to respond to those shifts in life-giving and healthy ways.
3. To seek to faithfully live out vows I have made – to God, to my husband, to my children (through the sacraments of baptism, marriage and dedication, as well as in my role as part of the Order of the Mustard Seed).
4. To embrace life, to embrace joy, to embrace everyday wonder, to embrace love.
5. To be anchored in my faith in Jesus, and to be guided by love and hope.

What is your why?

Here's how you can start to form your 'why':

1. Stream-of-consciousness writing. Set a timer for ten minutes, write the title 'My why' and then put pen to paper and just write. Don't pause, just let whatever is there come out; don't edit, just flow. Then you can read through and see if anything feels true. If it does, highlight it so that you can come back to it later.
2. Schedule in whatever time you can – half an hour to a whole day – to be alone and silent to pray about your why. Maybe go for a walk and then sit with a journal and see what comes up.
3. Talk to a good friend/leader/partner/spiritual director and run your ideas past them. Listen to their insights.
4. Once you have completed the first three tasks and done

anything else that helps you to think, see if you can write five sentences like the examples above. This isn't fixed but it's a great starting point. Then, I encourage you to keep them with this book, and as you begin to work through and form your rule of life, you can see if the practices you are thinking of doing will help you achieve your why.

OK, that introduction has been a lot! We've delved into the science of the brain, and we've explored our beginner's mind and our why. Now, let's head back to the birth of contemplative Christianity: to the desert mothers and fathers who fled the state religion of their day, to the monasteries and convents of religious orders, modern lay orders and the wild mystic poets. There's plenty of inspiration to be gathered from their stories before we begin to build our rule.

Monks, saints and mystics

Through their poetry, their lives, and their prayers, God played for us His music, which can still be heard today, hundreds of years later, for what a party the soul aflame creates.
St Francis, quoted by Daniel Ladinsky[7]

Looking back to look forward

We all have people who inspire us, some of them alive today and some from the distant past. We can learn from looking back, not only at our own life and experience, but at the lives and experiences of others. There are endless examples we could explore in this chapter, but I am going to draw from just a handful who provide broad insights into what it can look like to have a life devoted to God, and to a variety of rhythms and practices that sustain that devotion.

As you read through this brief glimpse into their lives, let the snapshots travel from your head to your heart. Whose life is speaking to you today? What is it that draws you to their story? Can you name it? Is it Julian's strategic choice to become an anchoress? Is it St John of the Cross's endurance to keep going through his dark night? Is it St Francis's devotion and bravery, literally stripping off everything that could hinder him (riches, societal standing, his own family, his own clothes!) and running after his values?

We will explore how different people from across different centuries with different characters and callings dedicated their lives to walking with God. Don't let this chapter just be about information and historical context. Yes, it is certainly that, and

---

7 D. Ladinsky, trans. (quoting St Francis), *Love Poems from God: Twelve Sacred Voices from the East and West* (London: Penguin Compass, 2002), p. xii.

that's important. But let it help you to plumb your own depths. I encourage you to allow these accounts to stoke the fire of curiosity as you explore what living a life deeply connected to God could look like. We need stories, we really do; they unlock doors within us! I wonder, what will be unlocked in you today as you read and take the time to reflect?

Activity

Put down this book and get really comfortable in your seat. Notice your body, notice your breath. Recognise and welcome the presence of God in which you are already immersed. Maybe place a hand over your heart – a physical representation of a deeper spiritual reality that you are connected to God. Spend a couple of minutes praying and inviting God to speak to you as you read. Pray that you will have eyes to see and that you will notice where the Spirit is leading you. You may want to start with these words of prayer: 'Kind and loving God, open my spiritual eyes and ears to be moved by these stories. What little bit of treasure do you have for me today, hidden within them? I release all sense of pressure and come like a child to be met by you through people who devoted their lives to pursuing you and your kingdom. Amen.'

Desert mothers and fathers

Before we get into specific individuals, let's look right back at the women and men often referred to as the desert mothers and fathers and see what we can glean.

When Christianity became the state religion of the Roman empire in AD 313, everything changed. For the first time, Christians weren't persecuted and could live without fear. But this meant that rather than being devoted to the radical ways of Christ, people could just be nominal Christians. This was now the done thing in society. It led to a lot of compromise in the ways people lived out their faith. Christianity doesn't mix well with power, and we have a long and colourful history to prove that. It has, however, always flourished on the margins.

Such compromise led to certain followers of Jesus fleeing to the outskirts of the towns and deep into the wilderness of the desert. This meant they could continue the radical way of living out their faith they had known before it became the state religion. Over time, some formed monastic communities of prayer, work and service and some withdrew further and lived as hermits.

Observing their lives can teach us a radical renunciation of all that can hinder us from a life of faith and show us how to commit to our values, whatever the cost. Just like the disciples before them, these people gave up everything to follow the way of Jesus.

This is an overview of some of the key figures and a couple of examples of principles we can take with us on our own journeys. Don't forget to read attentively to see what the Spirit might be revealing to you personally about their lives.

Here are some of the names of the desert mothers that we know:

- Amma Matrona
- Amma Sarah
- Amma Syncletica of Alexandria
- Amma Theodora

We know very little of these women, which is no shock really, given when they lived. Women aren't documented in much of our history, religious or otherwise. Amma Syncletica is known to have been a wise counsellor of the soul, and many of her sayings survive to this day: she taught that 'your life striving for the presence of God… is like a Paradise; it must be guarded by a flaming sword – of prayer and remembrance of God'.[8]

---

[8] A. Isaiah, *Matericon: Instructions of Abba Isaiah to the honorable nun Theodora* (Stafford, AZ:St. Paisius Serbian Orthodox Monastery, 2001), p. 61.

Faith Habits and How to Form Them

From what we do know, they lived simply, slowly and intentionally, which helped them to hear and discern God in their everyday lives. This is the key lesson I've taken from the women of the desert. When we live at the pace of our modern culture and are pulled in a million different directions, it's hard to hear the still, small voice of God that many of us yearn for. While we may not be able to flee to the literal wilderness like these desert Ammas, we can integrate practices of silence, solitude and stillness into our everyday lives and carry their inspiration and example with us into the modern day.

We have much more information on the men, but, again, this is just a snapshot of their lives and a couple of sayings. Here are the names of some of the most prominent:

- Anthony the Great
- Poemen
- Macarius of Egypt
- Moses the Black

Anthony moved to the desert about AD 270 and was known as the one who really got things going, although he isn't documented to be the first. By the time he died in 356, there were thousands of people living in the deserts of Egypt.

The desert fathers chose a life of extreme simplicity: all pleasures, luxuries and comforts were off the table. They focused on prayer and singing psalms, either living as hermits or in peaceful communities. Like the women, they attracted many who sought their wisdom, which they gave freely. A lot of the monastic orders that we know today drew heavily from their example. Here are just a couple of quotes:

> Go and sit in your cell, and your cell will teach you everything.
> Abba Moses[9]

---

9 J. Chittister, *Illuminated Life: Monastic Wisdom for Seekers of Light* (Maryknoll, NY: Orbis Books, 2000), p. 21.

> My book, O Philosopher, is the nature of created things, and whenever I want to read the word of God, it is right in front of me.
> St Anthony[10]

These quotes speak to me of quiet intentionality; of listening to the world around us, of listening to our lives and the God who inhabits them – and letting them be our teacher. In a world of more, more, more, this is important. Maybe the last thing we need is another teaching, another conference, another app, another gadget. Maybe the lesson here from the desert fathers is much like the opening quote of this book from Barbara Brown Taylor: '[we] have everything we need to begin.' God is already entirely present and we are already entirely enough. It's just a case of beginning to live intentionally with eyes to see and ears to hear God. Again, our rule will help us to live this out.

Questions for reflection
- What inspires you about the lives of the desert mothers and fathers?
- Is there anything about them that makes you feel uncomfortable or that you feel is no longer relevant?

Monastic orders – ancient and modern

There are many types of monastic orders from across the Protestant, Catholic and Orthodox traditions of Christianity. These are the most well known:

- Franciscan
- Carmelite

---

10 Chittister, *Illuminated Life*, p. 83.

- Benedictine
- Cistercian
- Carthusian
- Trappist

They vary greatly in purpose and the rules of life by which they live. But they share basic principles: some form of withdrawal, times of prayer and work, times of community, and times of silence and solitude. Essentially, they all take vows and live by a shared rule that is set by the order.

There are also very modern lay (non-clergy) monastic orders and new monastic communities that help ordinary folk living ordinary lives to do a version of the same thing. I have been a member of one of these for several years now. They helped me to craft my own personalised rule of life and to know that lots of other people around the world are doing the same – following the same values and practices but living them out in their own unique context. Here are a few modern lay orders:

- Northumbria community
- Community of Aiden and Hilda
- The Order of the Mustard Seed
- The Order of Sustainable Faith

From both versions of monastic communities, we can learn the value of not living an isolated faith: the value of entering more deeply into community with other Christians, helping our faith to grow and become deeper, beyond mere church attendance or a certain set of beliefs. We can see how having some set rhythms and practices can help form a trellis of support for our spiritual lives. We can also know that we are part of a very long tradition, right from the disciples of Jesus, who found ways to live rich spiritual lives among the trials and tribulations of their own generation.

Questions for reflection

- As you think about these more modern, lay forms of monastic communities and the more formal ones they come from, what inspires you about them?
- Is there something you can take from here into your own context to influence how you live in community?
- Is there anything about them that puts you off?

What can we learn from saints and holy people?

In one sense, we are all saints: 'But you are a chosen people, a royal priesthood, a holy nation, God's own people, in order that you may proclaim the excellence of him who called you out of darkness into his marvellous light' (1 Peter 2:9 NRSV). But in this context, I am referring to some of those who have been given this title officially by the Church after their death. These people were ordinary human beings living in a particular period of history, many of them a long time ago. It's important to not assign twenty-first-century culture and values to them. As I said, they were human. Remember that they made mistakes as we all do.

Some did particularly extraordinary things, while others led quiet lives. All suffered in one way or another. There is still much to be learned from looking at their lives: we can learn from their efforts to love God and seek a profound relationship with the Trinity, but I encourage you just to keep their humanity in mind as you read. I'm never going to be able to do this massive topic justice in a book this size, but I will point you to further reading if you are keen to delve deeper!

Julian of Norwich (1342–c.1416)

> He attributes no blame, out of love... Peace and love are always in us, being and working, but we are not always in peace and love. But he wants us to pay attention to this: that he is the foundation of our whole life in love.
> Julian of Norwich[11]

---
11 Julian of Norwich, *Revelations of Divine Love*, ch. 45, 'Who is Julian of Norwich', Julian of Norwich: https://julianofnorwich.org/pages/who-is-julian-of-norwich (accessed 20 January 2025).

Julian of Norwich was never actually declared a saint, but she was clearly a very holy person. From what we can piece together, Julian survived three waves of the Black Death that ravaged her hometown of Norwich. She lost many people she loved, including her father, husband and only daughter along the way. In May 1373, during a time of illness that was close to fatal, she received mystical visions of Christ, described then as 'shewings'. She later became what was known as an 'anchoress', which means she chose to withdraw from the world. She lived out her life physically bricked into a small room attached to a church, after being read the death rites. She committed to living a life of extreme simplicity and prayer in service to the Church.

Julian decided to die to her normal life and instead chose a life of prayer and meditation on her 'shewings'. She received people who came to her for prayer and wisdom at her window, much like the desert mothers and fathers who chose to live as hermits. She was in that room until she died some decades later.

There are so many things that draw me to Julian personally, but the thing I would love to emphasise is her ability to hold tension. If there was ever a person who could do this well, it was she. Some of her revelations directly opposed the teachings of the Church in her day, but she never let that fluster her. She simply held both and let it be a mystery. I think we all need a bit of that in our current cancel culture. What an example of humility and tolerance.

She is also an inspiration in prayer, risk, devotion, and commitment to the Church and the revelations she received. She was ingenious in becoming an anchoress as it allowed her to meditate on her 'shewings' without having the constant busyness of being a nun, or of getting married again, working and bearing more children. She also became a woman from whom people sought wisdom. Beloved by so many, she lived a long life, as well as being the first woman to write an autobiography – at great risk to herself and others.

Questions for reflection
- Is there an area of your life in which you could be inspired and helped by following Julian's example of holding tension and trusting God when you don't understand or can't see a solution? Is there anything else about her life that speaks to you?

St Francis of Assisi (1181–1226)

Lord, make me an instrument of your peace.
St Francis[12]

St Francis is a much beloved and fascinating character. He had a wealthy upbringing and did plenty of partying in his youth, but he met God in a dank prison cell after being captured in war and held for a year. He returned home and, soon after, left his status, family and riches to live a life of poverty and simplicity. He apparently handed his fine clothes back to his father in a public place, leaving himself naked, until the priest gave him a simple rough tunic that became his clothing. He embraced lepers. He preached in a way that meant ordinary people could really meet God, and he gained many followers, eventually forming the monastic order of Franciscan friars. He is even the official patron saint of ecology because of his love of nature and animals, to whom, it is reported, he also preached God's love! On his feast day, some churches still hold a special service for people to bring their pets to receive a blessing.

Francis is an example of following our values at all costs: an embodiment of the scripture of giving up mothers and brothers and worldly riches for the gospel.

---

12 J. Davis, D. McMingle and L. Muir, *The Gift of St Francis* (Leominster, Herefordshire: Gracewing, 2003), p. 121.

Question for reflection
- What is it about Francis's life that draws or challenges you?

St John of the Cross (1542–91)

For contemplation is naught else than a secret, peaceful and loving infusion from God, which, if it be permitted, enkindles the soul with the spirit of love...
St John of the Cross[13]

St John of the Cross is the ultimate paradox for our modern era. A priest, poet and reformer, he was part of the Carmelite order and, along with the well-known St Teresa of Ávila, stood up against what he believed were the wrongdoings of the religious order of his day and paid the price. He was brutally imprisoned and tortured by the Church for daring to speak out against them. However, as he suffered horribly in prison, he found a deep inner freedom and an ecstatic love of God. After escaping his awful, small prison cell, he took refuge and continued his work on reform and writing until his death. He is probably best known for his experience and writings on 'the dark night of the soul'.

For me, St John of the Cross is an example of trusting that after death comes the resurrection: an example of holding on to faith, hope and love in the midst of suffering and hatred.

Questions for reflection
- What draws you to St John of the Cross?
- What do you find challenging about his example?

---

13 St John of the Cross, *Dark Night of the Soul* (Dover Thrift Editions), trans. E. A. Peers (Mineola, NY: Dover Publications, Inc., 2003), p. 27.

St Teresa of Calcutta ('Mother Teresa', 1910–97)

I want you to love the poor, and never turn your back to the poor, for in turning your back to the poor, you are turning it to Christ.

Mother Teresa[14]

Mother Teresa was born in what is now known as North Macedonia but is known for her devoted life to the poor in Calcutta (now Kolkata), India, where she began her work by teaching and feeding street children. She and the Sisters of Mercy founded Nirmal Hriday, the home for the dying, which offered dignity and care to the poor, the rejected and those abandoned by society. Embodying the scripture 'what you do for the least of these you do for me', they felt that as they tended to the poor and the dying in the most difficult circumstances, they were tending to Christ himself. It was a true and profound example of self-abnegation, love and care of the poor. The sisters were also devoted in prayer, pausing their serving to pray five times a day.

My days as a working mum-of-four can be really busy and overwhelming, but I imagine less so than an average day for the Sisters of Mercy. Their dedication to pausing to pray inspires us all to find a few more moments in our day. As well as that devotion to prayer, Mother Teresa and her sisters are also an inspiration in their care for the poor and the needy. They gave up their lives for the lives of others.

---

14 Mother Teresa, 'Mother Teresa Acceptance Speech', The Nobel Prize: https://www.nobelprize.org/prizes/peace/1979/teresa/acceptance-speech/ (accessed 20 January 2025).

Question for reflection
- What is it about Mother Teresa and her sisters that has spoken to you?

St Ignatius of Loyola (1491–1556)

God dwells in me, bringing me into being, giving me life, feeling and understanding.
St Ignatius of Loyola[15]

St Ignatius of Loyola was born into a wealthy family and was one of thirteen children. While fighting in battle, he sustained life-changing injuries. During his long convalescence, he had two books to read, one on the life of Christ and one on the saints. He became captivated by the idea of God and decided to change his life. After a lot of exploration, learning and wrestling, he founded the Society of Jesus, more commonly known as the Jesuits, in 1534. In 1548, the Spiritual Exercises of St Ignatius of Loyola were officially recognised, although he had already been teaching them for many years. The Spiritual Exercises are made up of prayers and reflections with the goal of deepening the participants' relationship with God. They were traditionally done in an intensive format over thirty days in a monastery. Some people still do this, but more commonly a more manageable version is done over a period of about nine months and can be done from home.

Ignatius brought many gifts to the Church, but, for me, the greatest are the tools for spiritual formation. Practices and methods such as discernment and the examen have been life-changing for so

---

[15] D. Birchall SJ (ed.), 'Journey into Freedom: A retreat based on the Spiritual Exercises of Saint Ignatius Loyola', The Ignatian Spirituality Centre, Glasgow, in association with Pathways to God, Website, 2020: https://www.dunkelddiocese.co.uk/wp-content/uploads/2020/02/Lent%20Retreat%202020%20FINAL.pdf (accessed 20 January 2025), p. 15.

many people. He is also an example of devotion, tenacity, standing by your beliefs no matter the cost, and leadership.

Question for reflection
- What can you learn from the life of St Ignatius of Loyola?

St Catherine of Siena (1347–80)

> It could be said that God's foot is so vast that this entire earth is but a field on His toe... What then is not a sanctuary? Where then can I not kneel and pray at a shrine made holy by His presence?
> St Catherine of Siena[16]

Catherine was born to a family of twenty children. Accounts say that she had visions of Jesus and a desire to live a religious life from as young as six years old. She joined a Dominican lay group and lived a short but devoted life caring for everyone around her with great love, especially those in great need. She and her writings have remained very highly thought of, but it wasn't until 1970 that she was officially proclaimed a Doctor of the Church by the Pope.

Her life was a simple, devout and short one. She is an example to me of the Great Commission and the Great Commandment. She loved God and she loved others. Without fanfare, she loved and experienced Jesus deeply and gave that love away at every opportunity.

Question for reflection
- Sometimes when we think of saints, we think of the mystical and the magnificent. But how can this simple life of St Catherine of Siena speak to you today?

---

16 Ladinsky, *Love Poems from God*, p. 205.

The few saints that we have just explored together are mainly from hundreds of years ago. I want to finish with a couple of well-known monks from the past century. Both of these men contributed greatly to the current resurgence in the contemplative tradition within Christianity.

What can we learn from monks?

Thomas Merton (1915–68)

Our happiness consists in sharing the happiness of God, the perfection of His unlimited freedom, the perfection of His love.
Fr Thomas Merton[17]

Often referred to as the father of the modern contemplative movement, Thomas Merton was born in 1915 and became a Trappist monk in 1941. Fr Thomas wrote extensively on the contemplative tradition and non-violence, among other things. Many modern writers draw from his work, one of the most famous of which is *The Seven Storey Mountain*, which documents his spiritual journey. He worked in the civil-rights movement in the United States of America despite being criticised for doing so. He died prematurely in a freak accident, from being electrocuted in his room whilst on a trip in Thailand.

I am inspired by his devotion to following and standing up for what he believed even when others in his faith community failed to understand his actions.

Question for reflection
- What inspires you about the person or work of Thomas Merton?

---

17 T. Merton, *The Seven Storey Mountain* (San Diego: Harcourt Brace & Company, 1999), p. 409.

Thomas Keating (1923–2018)

The chief thing that separates us from God is the thought that we are separated from Him.
Thomas Keating[18]

Thomas Keating was a Trappist priest, an author and the founder of Contemplative Outreach, an organisation dedicated to resourcing people on the contemplative tradition and providing education and training. He is often referred to as the father of centering prayer. He worked on developing and equipping people in centering prayer and the programs for happiness, which I talked about earlier. His understanding of the intersection, in practice, of spirituality and psychology is incredible. He worked hard to equip the next generation in the contemplative path, holding training sessions at his monastery and teaching extensively. Just like many of the other wonderful people we have read about, Thomas sometimes had to stand up to his religious order. I have found his work to be utterly transformational and readily accessible. A lot of his video teachings are still available on YouTube, as well as his insightful books. His work *The Human Condition* is one of those tiny but mighty books that has me pausing and highlighting every other line. I highly recommend it.

Question for reflection

- What speaks to you from Thomas Keating's life and teachings?

We've only got space for a tiny snapshot of the history and legacy of the monastic tradition and the lives of some of its saints and monks. But I hope it has been enough to whet your appetite and to feel surrounded by a great cloud of witnesses as you embark on your own journey.

---

18 T. Keating, *Open Mind, Open Heart: The Contemplative Dimension of the Gospel*, 20th Anniversary Ed. (New York: Continuum, 2008), p. 33.

One thing in common

As we bring this section to a close, I want to point out one thing all these people had in common. They were all ordinary people who made a decision to commit deeply to being loved by and loving Jesus. Driven from this place of love, they followed him and his example, whatever the cost. We have all we need within us to embark on this journey ourselves. We, like them, are ordinary people with a desire for more of God in our lives.

We live in a world that tells us we need more of everything. It leaves us unsatisfied as we feel we never have enough. We never get to the impossible end goal; it's always just out of reach. The people who make money from our desire to want more make sure of that. Do you know that we have the technology to make a lightbulb that never needs replacing? But what kind of business model would that be? So, they adapted the design to make sure lightbulbs had a shelf life and people would come back as they would need replacing. There you have it: capitalism in a lightbulb!

Imagine the beauty industry telling women you are stunning and valued just as you are. Not really a moneymaker, is it? We do it to ourselves, too. I'll be able to make that change when the kids are older, when we get a bigger house, when so-and-so leaves my workplace, when my partner/relative/friend changes in this way or that way, when I finally get my act together about XYZ. And does that work? No. This is the human experience.

When we look at those who have chosen to live a radically different life, giving up a lot of the luxuries and trappings of culture and society, we see that they all share a desire for something deeper, more real and more true. Jesus was always telling us to wake up. To wake up to the deepest reality: that we are loved, that we are connected to God. And those who took that call seriously to move beyond the trappings of the ego/the false self/sin/whatever you want to call it – well, they spent their whole lives being humbled and having to wake up again and again. This is not the easy way out. This is hard. It was hard for Jesus and his followers, it was hard for the desert mothers and fathers, it was hard for the Benedictines, the Cistercians and Franciscans, the saints, and it's hard for us now. Every generation and culture has had its trappings. They may look different on the surface. Abba Anthony wasn't battling addiction to social media, but he will have had his own struggles – ones that made it seem necessary for him and countless others to flee to the desert.

Greed, pride, vanity, insecurity, comparison. They may have had different cultural and historical expressions, but their essence is the same. We all want and in fact need security and survival, affection and esteem, and power and control. None of us got all of them or perceived we got all of them in our formative years. Without that deep-felt sense of union with God, we spend our lives looking for what we already in fact have.

Religion hasn't always been the most helpful in this, either. The Church may not want to face it, but there are swathes of people who leave totally disillusioned under the weight of guilt and shame coming from what should be the freest place on earth. It's very sad.

Some people fled. They fled the trappings of their society to live a different way. To varying degrees, they gave up their possessions, their freedom to live lives of sheer individuality and choice, and many also gave up the chance to be married and have children, in order to devote themselves to God.

I believe they have become 'saints' and we still talk about them because something in their radical choices speaks deeply into our hearts and our essence. We know there's more. As the theologian and author Richard Foster said: '[We've] heard the call to deeper, fuller living. [We've] become weary of frothy experiences and shallow teaching… [We] long to launch out into the deep.'[19] For better or for worse, these guys launched. Their example can be a launchpad for us, too.

---

19 R. Foster, *Celebration of Discipline: The Path to Spiritual Growth* (London: Hodder & Stoughton, 2008), p. 3.

Part 2
THE PRACTICES

I pray that on your journey you continue to seek the God who is seeking you. When the world tries to squeeze you into its mold, break the mold! Step back from the busy and make some space for God through spiritual practices.
Adele Ahlberg Calhoun[20]

---

20 Ahlberg Calhoun, *Spiritual Disciplines Handbook*, p. 11.

How do I start?

It's been incredible looking back over the monastic tradition that has provided some foundation and inspiration for us and given us something real and tangible to build upon. But sometimes our ordinary lives can feel too far removed from the monastic or contemplative way of living. I have certainly felt that way over these past fifteen years. I wrestle with these thoughts in my daily life.

Living a life connected to God starts in the daily. It starts with the life we have right now and the person we are today. It starts and continues to be imperfect. But what matters is that we start – that we allow ourselves to fail, and that we start again. You don't need to wait for better circumstances or timing; you can trust the process of becoming, you just need to embark on the journey.

Spiritual practices are not an end in themselves. Although important, they are not the point of, or where we walk out our faith. They are incredible tools that help us and position us to live a life of faith, and that occurs in our everyday, ordinary lives: in work meetings, in our neighbourhoods and within our families; in our conversations, our thoughts and a thousand small choices to walk with Jesus and walk the way of love every day.

> So here's what I want you to do, God helping you: Take your everyday, ordinary life – your sleeping, eating, going-to-work, and walking-around life – and place it before God as an offering.
> Romans 12:1 MSG

Whether you are an early bird, a night owl or some sort of permanently exhausted pigeon, it doesn't matter. Some of you are already engaging in a life full of practices, while others only manage a desperate prayer to stop themselves yelling at the kids for leaving every light on all the time. Regardless of your starting point, I invite you to turn towards yourself with love and acceptance and take a deep breath. You are beloved and enough just as you are. It is from here that we begin. Beloved. Accepted. Enough.

Pause. I invite you to lay a hand over your heart and pray this prayer:

God of love, I thank you that I can come to you just as I am. Help me to see myself as you do, entirely beloved, accepted and enough.
Amen.

It's taken me a lot of time to be able to pray prayers like that and actually believe them deep in my being. It can be a bit like forgiveness; sometimes it starts with a decision and an intention, and finally our feelings catch up.

After beginning to establish this posture as beloved people, I'm afraid we have to get practical! I invite you to spend some time thinking of what your daily life looks like at the moment, making a kind of non-judgemental inventory. I strongly encourage you not to skip over this part. It's pointless gathering more information if you don't have any idea of how and when you can integrate it into your actual life. I've answered the questions for you below, partly by way of example and partly because who doesn't enjoy a bit of a nose into other people's lives? Grab a journal and let's go!

What daily practices do you already do?

- The Ignatian Spiritual Exercises in the morning, which include some *lectio* and journalling. My centering prayer and movement have both taken a back seat to accommodate this

recently. It annoys me I can't fit it all in – in the beginning I tried, but the reality of having four kids and a job kicked in.
- Reading the New Zealand Anglican alternative version of the Lord's Prayer.
- Examen and writing in my gratitude journal before bed.

What are your current immovable commitments?

- Teaching schedule
- Family and church commitments
- The Ignatian Spiritual Exercises (every day for nine months)

What is your current capacity and availability?

- One hour in the morning – when I actually get up!
- Thirty minutes before bed – when I'm not playing solitaire on my phone.
- Twenty minutes most afternoons – when I'm not distracted by anything and everything.

Does anything in your life need to be reduced to make space? (Please be realistic!)

I get so bored of this sticky problem, but too much time on my phone.

Late nights – at my stage of life with changing hormones, these have a real impact. If I don't go to bed on time, I don't get up early enough for my practices and my energy is affected all day, and then I don't sleep well. It's a vicious cycle I just don't have time for!

Allowing the fear of judgement from other people to stop me putting good boundaries in place – even though I know the path

I'm called to walk means boundaries other people may not need but I definitely do. Even when I know it's the right thing to do... I still struggle. Being a human is hard sometimes!

What times of day work well for you to integrate practices?

For me it's the mornings, pre-7 a.m., and right before bed. With my own business and four children between ten and seventeen, other times of day just aren't reliable. I do get micro-moments, but I grab these when I can, and I'm not able to plan them.

Are your weekends different from your weekdays?

Yes, Saturdays are my Sabbath. No alarm and a family day. On Sundays I go to church in the morning, but I have some free time in the afternoon.

Do you put personal space or others first?

I land on the take-up space/self-oriented side of this. So, it's really important for me that I consider others when planning. My husband lands on the side that prioritises everybody else. So, he needs encouragement to take up space. Being aware of this helps us to plan together as a couple.

Who can you share your plan with?

My spiritual director and my husband.
OK, your turn!

Daily practices

Now that we've spent some time reflecting, let's begin to explore some of the spiritual practices. We're going to look at a selection of daily practices that are used right across the breadth of the Christian tradition. Some you might feel comfortable and familiar with, some might not appeal to you or you may even totally disagree with – that's OK; take from the practices those which are helpful to you, and if you see something you don't like, just skip over it. If we ever want unity across the Church, which Jesus seemed pretty keen on by the way, it's important to move against the cancel culture so prevalent in our world right now. Some of them are well-known, classical practices such as *lectio divina*; others less so. The less traditional practices are more about ordinary things we can do with a prayerful intention, such as prayerful walking. I have used all of them with varying degrees of success and commitment at different times over the last decade. Please don't worry; this is not a list that you have to complete! Instead, I encourage you to read through them slowly and prayerfully. Where do they produce an inner spark? Which ones might God be leading you towards right now? In light of the questions you answered above, begin to think about how you might consider gently and realistically integrating one or two of these into your everyday life. You could then try them out for a couple of weeks and see what you think. If you find they aren't a good fit, try something different until you find practices that work for you. It may be a bit of trial and error at first, and that's totally OK. You may even find you don't need to add much in, just a reframing or adaption of practices you already do. Countless entire books have been written on each of these practices, so this is just a brief introduction; you can find further

Lectio divina

The first practice I want to explore with you is a personal favourite: *lectio divina*. *Lectio* is a beautiful, sacred practice. It is a way of reading attentively, inviting and allowing the text to both speak to us and read us. At its essence it is saying, 'You can be met by the Spirit of God here.' Therefore, when you come to it, you are saying: 'I can be touched and met and known here in this sacred reading.'

It sounds lofty and mystical, doesn't it? I mean, it is, I guess. But it's also simple and accessible. *Lectio divina*, simply put, is a tool for being met by God in and through your reading. I invite you to put yourself in the imaginary scenario I've outlined below. I'll show you a way you can approach the ancient practice, and hopefully it will bring it down to earth for you.

You've had a busy day and are feeling a bit done in. Life has been grinding you down and you just need to get away from everything for a minute. You have the sense that you have something on, but you can't quite remember what it is. Then suddenly you realise you have a dinner date with your best friend and your spirits lift. You know you have some time coming up where you can be yourself – where you can be seen for who you are at your essence, not how you've maybe been acting in your stress or upset. You know you will be able to share and it will be understood. You know your trusted friend will have words to help you, that their very presence will help you see who you are and what to do that little bit more.

Close friends are amazing; they are one of the ways God comes to us. Scripture and sacred reading can be a similar way in which God comes to us, as that living friend. I didn't always experience the Bible in this way. In fact, I spent years struggling with it. But I've learned thanks to the contemplative path in general and *lectio* specifically that God can be met there. The Bible talks about its words being alive and active, sharper than a two-edged sword (Hebrews 4:12). For something to be alive and active in this present moment, by definition, it needs to be breathing now. That means the Bible, as well as being a book of historical accounts, letters, wisdom and poetry, is also living and moving. This is only possible through the activity and movement of the Holy Spirit.

If you want to, you can come to this practice like you would your best friend: relaxed and ready, expecting to be met. Will it always be mind-blowing and fantastic? No. Is every conversation with your friend like that? Or sometimes, is it more like a moan over the weather or a smile over a shared sunset? Regardless, isn't it still good to hang out and be in their presence?

Now you've understood the heart, here are the facts: *lectio divina* is an ancient practice dating back to the sixth century AD, used traditionally in monasteries and presided over by priests. It is a sacred way of reading and engaging, traditionally with Scripture, but it can also be used with other devotional writing and poetry. Rather than reading for information, you are reading more for transformation – allowing, if you like, the text to read you. I find it works best with a small amount of text, and classically it has four stages:[21]

- Stage 1: Reading (*lectio*). Read a Scripture passage listening with the 'ear of your heart'. What word or phrase captures your attention? Repeat it gently.
- Stage 2: Reflecting (*meditatio*). Reflect on and relish the words. Be attentive to what speaks to your heart.
- Stage 3: Responding (*oratio*). As listening deepens, allow responses to arise spontaneously – praise, thanksgiving, questions, petitions.

---

21 'Lectio Divina', Contemplative Outreach: https://www.contemplativeoutreach.org/lectio-divina-contemplation/ (accessed 20 January 2025).

- Stage 4: Resting in (*contemplatio*). Simply 'be with' God's presence as you open to deeper meanings of the word of God for you.

I love Christine Valters Paintner's alternative names for the categories: Shimmering, Savouring, Summoning and Stilling.[22]

If you don't have time for all the stages, or find them overwhelming, you can engage with the essence of the practice by approaching your reading prayerfully and reflectively, seeing what the Spirit might be saying to you through it. I always find it helpful to have a journal on hand to note down any thoughts or observations. For me, *lectio divina* would be a morning practice, but it can of course be done at any time of day. As it is a small amount of Scripture that I am delving into more deeply, I find it sticks with me through my day, and it can continue to speak hours later. It is such a wonderful, accessible practice for anybody to do; I hope you have fun with it.

Centering prayer

> Centering prayer is a consenting and surrendering to God. The spiritual journey does not require going anywhere because God is already present and within us.
> Thomas Keating[23]

> Between stimulus and response there is a space. In that space is the power to choose our response. In our response lies our growth and our freedom.
> Viktor E. Frankl[24]

---

22 C. Valters Paintner, 'The Sacred Art of Reading the World – Lectio Divina as a Life Practice', Abbey of the Arts, 19 February 2017: https://abbeyofthearts.com/blog/2017/02/19/the-sacred-art-of-reading-the-world-lectio-divina-as-a-life-practice-a-love-note-from-your-online-abbess/ (accessed 20 January 2025).

23 Keating, *Open Mind, Open Heart*, p. 20.

24 V. E. Frankl, *Man's Search for Meaning* (London: Penguin, 2020).

Faith Habits and How to Form Them

You know how a lot of contemplative people are gentle and calm, measured and mellow? Well, I'm not like that at all. I'm more like a freight train, a friendly, smiley one… but a freight train, nonetheless. I'm full of ideas and fire and fears and hopes and disappointments. I open my eyes and my mind is on. There have been many an early morning when I've come downstairs excited, relaying a wild idea to my husband, who's just trying to come round with his second cup of coffee. I need every bit of help I can get to stay present, to let go and to grow that space between stimulus and response. Enter centering prayer.

Centering prayer is a wonderful form of meditation. Meditation helps to bring us into the present moment and builds a deep inner awareness in us. Centering prayer was developed and became popularised in the 1970s by Fr Thomas Keating and a small handful of other monks. Fr Thomas could see how much other Eastern religions and traditions had advanced in this area. In a brave and controversial move, he began learning from teachers of various other types of meditation, such as transcendental. Centering prayer was soon born and developed a humble but committed following.

It is no exaggeration to say that centering prayer changed my life. I'm also not exaggerating when I say I find my practice today as difficult as my first practice several years ago. I never want to do it. I hate being still and 'unproductive'. For me there is nothing fun about it. The fact that I never get any 'better' at it hurts my ego and I find it boring. After that glowing introduction, I bet you can't wait to get started! I also predict some of you are asking, if you find it so difficult, why on earth do you do it?

I do it because it is transforming me and I know it works. I see the fruit of it off my meditation cushion and in my everyday life. I do it because I need all the help I can get staying in the present moment. This practice helps me to notice when I'm distracted and fragmented. Vitally, it's helping me to think before I speak (at least some of the time). It makes me realise when I'm mindlessly daydreaming off into fantasy land or worrying fruitlessly about things out of my control. Centering prayer helps me remember I'm connected to God and that God is always present. It's worth every boring, ego-crushing minute.

In our non-stop, instant-results culture I think it's the perfect antidote to the demands of our age. Fancy a go? Here's how to get started:

- Step 1: Choose a sacred word as the symbol of your intention to consent to God's presence and action within.
- Step 2: Sitting comfortably and with eyes closed, settle briefly and silently introduce the sacred word as the symbol of your consent to God's presence and action within.
- Step 3: When engaged with your thoughts, return ever-so-gently to the sacred word.
- Step 4: At the end of the prayer period, remain in silence with eyes closed for a couple of minutes.[25]

Here are some examples of sacred words or short phrases: Jesus, YHWH, Lord, love is here, I'm here, presence.

All the classic instructions will insist on twenty minutes twice a day as minimum practice. Although this is optimal and will rapidly increase the strength of your inner observer and your ability to notice and discern your behaviour, it could also be a heavy start for some people. Unless you do well with jumping straight in, I think it can be kinder to slowly build up. If you feel drawn to this, why not consider five or ten minutes once a day and then increase your time bit by bit? It's also helpful to meet with other people and practise; even though you're sitting together in silence, there is definite encouragement in it. If you can't find a local group or a friend, there are some lovely online communities you can join.

---

25 'Centering Prayer', Contemplative Outreach: https://www.contemplativeoutreach.org/centering-prayer-method (accessed 20 January 2025)

Liturgical prayer

My secret is very simple: I pray.
Mother Teresa[26]

Depending on your tradition, you may or may not be familiar with liturgical prayer. Simply put, they are prayers in the words of others, often used in church settings. Some traditions use them all the time, others from time to time, and some almost never. I came from the 'almost never' camp. In my past, prayers were always 'spirit-led', generally long and in gathered settings. They were often filled with emotion or involved lots of people talking at once. That meant that for me, liturgical prayer was grounding and novel. I have heard mixed thoughts from friends who grew up in very liturgical churches; some love them, and some can find them a bit religious and empty. I guess this is one of those ones where you have to figure it out and ask the question, is this helpful for me?

There is a traditional liturgical calendar that has set scriptures for every day that you can follow. There are also many wonderful modern examples of pre-written prayer books you can either follow daily or dip in and out of. Some of my personal favourites are a variation of the Lord's Prayer in the New Zealand Anglican prayer book, the *Every Moment Holy* books and the Celtic *Daily Prayer* book.[27]

There are lots of reasons to pray with the words of others and to tap into ancient rhythms of prayer. If we only ever use our own words, then everything is through our perspective, including our limiting beliefs, prejudices and field of vision. Including prayers by

---

26 M. Teresa, *No Greater Love* (Novato, CA: New World Library, 1997), p. 3.

27 D. K. McKelvey, *Every Moment Holy, Volume I: New Liturgies for Daily Life* (Nashville, TN: Rabbit Room Press, 2021); The Northumbria Community, *Celtic Daily Prayer: Inspirational prayers & readings from the Northumbria Community* (London: Collins, 2005).

other people can be enlightening and balancing. To be honest, it also gives us a break from producing prayers ourselves. There have been many times in recent years when the words of others have carried and inspired me, giving language to things that I couldn't at the time. It's amazing how God can use the prayers of others to help us find connection and presence.

Is there a way you could integrate this liturgical prayer into a practice you already do? Is there a certain saint that inspires you? You could maybe pray one of their prayers as a starting point.

Journalling

Oh journalling, where would I be without you?! My beloved practice. People often ask if I'm an internal or external processor. Well, I'm both; I have my own category I call the hyper-processor. My mind can be just non-stop. Not only do I need time and space to process internally, I also need people to talk to and process externally. On top of that, I have journalling. That's where I mainly process my life with God. It's a place I go and unleash all my thoughts, fears, worries, wrestles, celebrations, decisions and hopes.

I don't know what I would do without it. A good friend of mine did a ten-day silent retreat in Thailand and she wasn't allowed her journal. The thought of it makes me sweat… I once did a three-day silent retreat and wrote fifty-four pages in mine!

There are different ways of prayer journalling, and it's good to experiment to find what works for you. As with all the practices, some might work better in different seasons of your life. Here are a few ideas to get you started:

- You might want to follow specific prompts. Feel free to look some up online, or create your own. Here are a few to spark your imagination:

Faith Habits and How to Form Them

Start-of-the-day prompts

1. What are my hopes for today?
2. What is coming up in my day that I specifically want to remember God's abiding presence for? This could be something joyful or challenging. Either way, you want to experience the alongside presence of God with more intention.
3. How am I entering this day? Emotionally, physically, spiritually?
4. What could I do to show someone else how loved they are today?

End-of-the-day prompts

1. How did I meet God today?
2. What am I grateful for today?
3. What was hard today?
4. What have I seen in the life of another or the world around me that I want to bring to God in prayer?

- Or you might want to address your prayer to God and then use imaginative prayer to journal the response.
- You might want to use your journal to log your emotional, physical, mental and spiritual health and observations, and then reflect to notice patterns.
- You might want to use it to document your prayer requests or your blessings.

You can use it however you would like to, but I encourage you to process and to write your prayers in some way at least some of the time. It's so lovely to have something to look back on because it's so easy to forget the small daily movements of God and our own hearts. It's those things that make up our life. It's precious to have them recorded.

The examen

> The Daily Examen is a technique of prayerful reflection on the events of the day in order to detect God's presence and discern his direction for us.
>
> IgnatianSpirituality.com[28]

The examen is an incredible reflective practice. It's a tool to help you see both God and your own heart more clearly. It fosters discernment in your life – to see patterns of behaviour and struggles, as well as the gifts and blessings of God. As the name suggests, it's the practice to help you cultivate an examined life.

The examen was developed by St Ignatius, who I mentioned in part one. A lot of the spiritual formation tools we have in our hands today are down to him. Everyone in his religious order had to practise the examen twice a day. Ignatius felt it grew essential discernment and honesty in his men. He also believed the examen was a gift directly from God, and that God wanted as many people as possible to benefit from it.[29]

The examen is about noticing the consolations and desolations within our day. According to Larry Warner in his book *Journey with Jesus*, '[Consolation is] a deep connection with God that does not necessarily have anything to do with emotions.' On the flip side, he said: '[Desolation can be described as] a disconnection with God that does not necessarily have anything to do with emotions.'[30]

A further description from the book that I have found helpful is:

---

[28] 'The Daily Examen', IgnatianSpirituality.com: https://www.ignatianspirituality.com/ignatian-prayer/the-examen/ (accessed 20 January 2025).

[29] 'The Daily Examen', IgnatianSpirituality.com.

[30] L. Warner, *Journey with Jesus: Discovering the Spiritual Exercises of Saint Ignatius* (Downers Grove, IL: IVP Books, 2010), pp. 300–01.

> Consolation is an outflow of your interior movement toward God, while desolation has to do with interior movement away from God, regardless of your feelings of pain or peace, comfort or confusion. Think of the focus of your life as being a computer screen. A simple way to remember the difference between consolation and desolation is this: consolation means that God is on the computer screen, while desolation means that God is not on the computer screen. The critical question becomes not 'what am I feeling?' but 'who is on my screen?'
> Larry Warner[31]

The examen gets to the heart of things and helps us to discern. As Jesus taught, true outworking of faith isn't our outward acts but our inward hearts. For example, what is sin for one isn't sin for another. Please allow me a slight digression on sin, since I brought it up. 'Sin' can be a heavy word for some, especially if you've been around preaching that has made you feel 'less than' because of it. For those who shy away from the word because of feelings of guilt and shame, I would love to take this opportunity to reframe sin. Put simply, sin is where we struggle the most. It's where we need the most help and the most love, and it is exactly where Jesus meets us full of grace and compassion. Among its many gifts, the examen can help us name our sin and notice patterns. This isn't to make us feel shame, but so we can grow and be healed from the brokenness. It's a beautiful, hopeful and redemptive process when taught and practised from a place of love. Here's a story from my life, to help illustrate what I mean…

I decided recently I wanted to get some portraits done for my fortieth birthday. I wanted to celebrate the body I have, just as it is at this stage in my life. I knew just the lady to ask; we dreamed up together the kind of images I wanted, taken on black-and-white film,

---

31 Warner, *Journey with Jesus*, p. 113.

no editing, photos that captured me just as I am. I was very excited. By now, you've probably realised… once I get an idea in my head, the next step is action. Patience is not my most prominent virtue. When I realised my photographer friend was going to be in town a few weeks later for a mutual friend's wedding, I jumped straight in and booked her for the day before the wedding. Did I mention that I was a bridesmaid in that wedding? And that my husband was officiating? In fact, it was the first wedding he ever officiated. I was keenly aware of this, and I had the slightest glimmer of guilt as I booked it in… but I quickly dismissed my concerns.

However, that evening when I did my examen practice, I came face to face with the fact that this was an untimely and selfish decision. These photos could be done at any time. The examen helped me to name and notice something that needed to be addressed. At this point, I should have cancelled, but instead I double-checked with Jon that it was OK. He said it was – as I knew he would. That way I appeased my guilt, and I didn't have to miss out!

A few days later, I practised the examen once again, and as I was asking God to search my heart, the photo session came floating back into my consciousness. This time, I was finally ready to see it for what it was: a desolation. I knew I really needed to be available in case my family or my friend needed me before the wedding, and the photos were not urgent. I consequently rescheduled the shoot and regained my peace. I experienced consolation on a soul level, even though it meant choosing to let go of getting my own way, and it didn't 'feel' good.

For me, this might have become a 'sin'. As I am naturally a person who puts herself first and easily takes up all the space, I almost went my own way, led by false self instead of my true self and God's love. I am now able to relay that story with no hint of shame, because I've done the work and I know where it comes from in my story. I always lean towards sorting my needs out, because it makes me feel safe. It's an area I need to continue to work on, to be met by grace to make a better choice. But with the help of a practice like the examen, I am able to notice the behaviour and be transformed. In this case, I eventually made a better choice because of my daily practice of the examen.

We need practices like the examen because they help us to see clearly. This is discernment: to perceive the truth of something at its essence. The examen leads us into our own heart and the healing that God wants to bring. It gives us time to pay attention, to notice patterns, to hear whispers, to be honest, to see the movements of God in our lives. It is a life-transforming practice and it's so easy to do! Life isn't easily categorised into two boxes, 'right' and 'wrong'. That's why we need discernment.

When it comes to practising the examen, there are many variations and resources available. I encourage you to do some research and find the one that sits well with you. My favourite is one I wrote for teenagers when I was introducing the practice at a youth camp. They found it so helpful in processing their days that one evening they all sat and copied the instructions out of my journal. Even though I am not a teenager, there's something just so accessible about this version.

Here's how to go about it:

1 Invite – Invite God into a time of reflection; invite the leading of the Holy Spirit as you journey back over your day.
2 Gratitude – As you scan back over your day, notice where you sensed the goodness or presence of God. This might be a direct experience or something you observed. If you aren't sure how to start, I find the fruits of the Spirit a good way to frame it. Where did you notice love, joy, peace, patience, kindness, goodness, faithfulness, gentleness or self-control? (Galatians 5:22)
3 What was hard? – What was something you struggled with today? Maybe you felt the perceived disconnection or absence

of God. Although we know there is nowhere we can go outside of God's presence (Psalm 139), it doesn't always feel that way. For this, I find looking at the opposites of the fruits of the Spirit a helpful tool to frame it.

4 Say sorry – Is there anything you want to repent for? Remember that repentance is beautiful too, and it's not about feeling guilty. It's a chance to turn from desolation and go in the direction of God and your truest, most whole self. It is a chance to be transformed.

5 Lay down and consecrate – Lay down everything from your current day and receive God's grace and love for you, remembering you are loved just as you are. Look ahead briefly at tomorrow, consecrate it to God and remember God's presence will be in and through all things of your day, known and unknown.

Does the examen seem like something you would like to include in your day? As you reflect on this, think about why and why not.

Breath prayer

In the early days of parenting when I had three boys under six and I was pregnant, I no longer knew which way was up. None of my pre-motherhood practices worked anymore. I was too tired to read my Bible, I couldn't pray with friends without being interrupted, and I rarely got to sit in church and listen to anything. This was before I knew about contemplative practices. I didn't know where to turn. I missed the spirituality I used to have, and none of my peers seemed to have any answers. The message I heard was that raising kids was your spiritual life now. In some ways I would say that is true; there is no sacred/secular divide. Our ordinary lives are where we meet God; everything can become an act of prayer, probably nothing more so than laying down your preferences to tend to the needs of your child. That said, it doesn't mean we can't find practices that tether us and keep us sane and connected in any busy season of life. Some of you may be right in the midst of a frantic season right now, and I want to tell you there is plenty you can participate in. Will it look the same? No. Will it still be wonderful? Yes.

An idea came to me one day during this period, when I was walking like a zombie towards one of the boys' cots to put a dummy back in: short sharp prayers. I could no longer sit in prayer meetings, but I could say a few words over and over again. These were breath prayers – an ancient practice going as far back as the fourth century AD. I, however, thought I'd invented them! I had no one to teach me about these practices back then; they just weren't present in the Christian community I was part of. Don't worry, I've now fully accepted they weren't my original idea!

Breath prayer is where you form a prayer using a few simple words, then repeat them in time with your breath. You may want to use a timer and do one, two or five minutes. The traditional breath prayer, or earliest version we know of, is often referred to as the Jesus Prayer, which originated from the Egyptian desert in the sixth century AD:

Inhale: Jesus Christ
Exhale: Have mercy on me (a sinner)

You can use that if it resonates with you, or you can create breath prayers yourself. You can use portions of Scripture, names of God, promises of God, or just general prayers. Here are some of my favourites:

Inhale: I am always
Exhale: In your presence

Inhale: You are
Exhale: Faithful

Inhale: You are closer
Exhale: Than my breath

Inhale: I rest
Exhale: In you

You can use them in lots of different ways: at set times of prayer, in the shower, when feeding a baby, at times of worry or stress. Again, there is so much versatility; you could say them out loud or pray them in your head. If you practise this earlier in the day, the words have the opportunity to come up as you live through your day, which can be nourishing.

Prayer postures

We find lots of prayer postures in the Bible. Different traditions use different postures, but they are all available to all of us. It can be nice to think of postures that embody or reflect the attitude of your heart in that time of prayer. Open palms are commonly used as they symbolise surrender. Raised arms indicate praise, and a hand on your heart can help to remember the closeness of God. Lying prostrate signals awe; swaying helps you enter into a moment of prayer or worship. You might do some of these automatically, but the more intention we put behind them, the more meaning they can grow to have.

I love to place my hands over my heart and move them lightly around that space as I begin to pray. It's part of my ritual of entering into prayer. I use the touch to remind me of God's closeness to me and the reality of that, sometimes intangible, but very real connection.

Which prayer posture appeals to you? Are there any you already do? Is there a way to integrate one into something you already do to deepen your experience?

Intuitive movement

Unlike your mind, which can be anywhere, your body is always right where you are. When we use our bodies and include them in our spiritual practices, it's another fantastic tool to help us stay present. They help up to move from thinking about an experience to actually having one. It can be anything from the simplest upturned palm to dancing in pure abandonment. There is movement suitable for every situation and every type of person. Unless movement comes really naturally to you, this might take some practice and experimentation to find things that work for you.

One way to give intuitive movement a go is finding a quiet space, putting on some music that helps you feel connected to God and just starting to move. Try beginning either standing, seated or down on your hands and knees. Imagine the Holy Spirit within your heart and all around you. Begin to move in any way that feels natural to you; your movements can be big or small, fast or slow. Allow yourself the chance to fully enter your heart and your body. Don't worry about what it looks like and don't try to 'do it right'; just let your body flow and feel. This is a way of being with God and fostering connection. You may find after doing it certain prayers and thoughts come to mind, or nothing may happen. When you are in a relationship with someone, there doesn't need to be outcomes of time spent together – you just spend time with them because you love them and you want to. Your relationship with God is the same. Why not be brave and give it a go?

Walking

Walking, for those who are able, is a wonderful way to spend time with God. When we walk, it boosts our brains and helps us to process our thoughts and emotions.[32] I don't know how many times

---

[32] F. Jabr, 'Why Walking Helps Us Think', *The New Yorker*, 2 September 2014: https://www.newyorker.com/tech/annals-of-technology/walking-helps-us-think (accessed 20 January 2025).

I've felt stuck or overwhelmed, gone for a walk and felt better on my return.

It can be used to simply soak in the outside world, to pray through things in our heads or to listen to God. Even a really quick walk on your lunch break or after dinner can become a sacred practice that increases your connection to God as well as your personal well-being. The difference between this and a normal walk is the intention to open yourself to the presence of God as you walk. Do you have a time you could include a prayerful walk into your day?

Swimming/running

Swimming and running are two other bilateral movements that, like walking, are good for the brain and processing. Performing them at a slow to moderate pace allows for prayer, and when I say allows for prayer I don't necessarily mean prayer with words, although you can do that. You can just be open to the presence of God as you do the activity, or you could be in a posture of listening or just creating space for receptivity. Are these activities that interest you?

Mindful movement and prayer

Five years ago I began offering online classes that combined two of my loves, contemplative prayer and gentle Pilates-based movement. Two years ago it evolved into an online community called The Prayer Orchard, where we now practise together three times a week. Taking some of the other practices offered in this book such as breath prayer and the examen and combining them with movement and breathing can create a wonderful embodied experience.

What are your thoughts on integrating prayer, breath and movement as a way of becoming more present to God in prayer? If you fancy a go, I invite you to try this simple movement and prayer combination for three rounds. From either sitting or standing, inhale and sweep your arms out to the sides and over your head, praying the words 'I am always'. Then exhale, bringing the arms back down praying the words 'in your presence'. For a full session, why not join me in The Prayer Orchard!

Chanting

This is not a common practice in any Christian communities I've been part of, but my exposure to chanting was first through a wonderful spiritual director who specialised in embodied practices. A gloriously wild, committed follower of Christ, she taught me the simple practice of chanting 'amen' ten times as part of my morning practices. I find it a brilliant way to help me to be present. Plus, the intention behind it was really important; I was saying 'amen' to whatever God would invite me into that day. This is a great posture to put your heart into at the beginning of the day. As my friend Jill Weber says, the answer is 'yes, God', now what's the question?

On a practical note, I live in a house full of people. It is rarely empty and chanting is a loud activity for the early morning! It's also a slightly awkward practice for when you're out and about. I find the shower or the car the best place for it. Could chanting play a part in your day?

Mini rituals

> Ritual – a way of doing something in which the same actions are done in the same way every time.
> *The Cambridge Dictionary*[33]

A lot of our lives are lived on autopilot. We all have a lot of rituals already, even if we don't recognise them. Mini rituals, such as

---

[33] 'ritual', *The Cambridge Dictionary*: https://dictionary.cambridge.org/dictionary/english/ritual (accessed 20 January 2025).

lighting a candle, stepping out and smelling the fresh air, a specific way of preparing a drink and lighting a fire, can all become meaningful prayerful practices. They would probably fall under the category of 'non-classical' disciplines. At first glance they may not seem very spiritual, but like anything, they become spiritual if used intentionally.

You may also have heard of 'habit stacking'. The idea is that you attach a habit to something you already do. Currently I am buying a certain food from a country involved in a war and praying for that nation every time I eat it. Non-classical disciplines are perfect for this kind of practice. Here are some ideas:

Making a hot drink

Could you slow it down? You could use a favourite mug, and make sure it's the only thing you are doing – not also scrolling through your phone or emptying the dishwasher at the same time. Incredibly, when we slow down and give the task in front of us our full attention, it doesn't waste time. The space of waiting for a kettle to boil gives time to pray or just be quiet, to fully embody the simple moment.

Stepping outside

As you begin your day, or maybe before you have lunch, could you step outside for a minute? Use your senses, look around you, smell the fresh air, feel the temperature, touch a plant? Take a moment to recognise and acknowledge God.

Breathing

At any point in the day – before entering prayer, before a meal, after a meeting – could you pause and take three to five slow deep breaths? Reorient yourself to the present moment and to God.

Lighting a candle

Candles have been used for centuries. They link us to a simpler time. They link us to ancient church practices. You can light a candle to orient you to prayer and to the light of Christ. It's a particularly powerful act when you have no words, or you can't find the light or hope in a situation. My husband often lights one candle to represent the light of Christ and then lights a second candle from the first to remind him that the light of Christ is within him, too.

The beautiful thing about these simple embodied practices is they help you to be really present, engaging your body. There is so much creative freedom under this category to do things that make your heart come alive and connect to God. What simple things could you build into your day? What do you already do that you could adapt and do with more intentionality?

Intercession

It won't have escaped your notice that there's a lot going on in the world right now. There probably always has been, but the difference is that we are exposed to much more of the pain these days. In years gone by, we would only be aware of what was happening locally, then maybe when the town crier would come around, or we would read the weekly newspaper. These days, the whole world is in our pocket all the time and it's a lot for our souls to bear.

Intercession is when we pray for others. In Claire Gilbert's fictional book about Julian of Norwich, *I Julian*,[34] she too becomes overwhelmed by all the concerns that come to her cell. Gilbert imagines Julian silently handing each of the people and all her concerns to Jesus and their being absorbed into his body… what a practice!

---

34 C. Gilbert, *I, Julian: The fictional autobiography of Julian of Norwich* (London: Hodder and Stoughton, 2023).

If you'd like to practise intercession, you could use a globe or a map and pray over the different countries. You could read the newspaper and pray through the needs you see. You could also join a prayer group at a local church or go prayer walking around your town, praying for schools, services and businesses. However you choose to do it, finding a way to pray for other people, local and global, is a great thing to do and include in our daily practices. What's your favourite way to pray for others?

Which practices are you drawn to?

That was your whistle-stop tour of some of my favourite daily practices, and it is by no means an exhaustive list. Did any stand out to you? Are there any that you already practise? Any you want to start practising? Make a note of these as we'll come back to them when we pull all of this together in your 'rule of life'.

I'll add a final note in this section to say that a lot of these practices are solitary. I by no means think the Christian life is a solitary one; it's just that the daily practices tend to be individual activities. They are things we maybe do early in the morning, last thing at night or on car rides or in our lunch break. Community practices come up more in other sections of the book; these are wonderful because part of the fun is having others to share the journey with.

> Kindred spirits are not so scarce as I used to think. It's splendid to find out there are so many of them in the world.
> L. M. Montgomery, *Anne of Green Gables*[35]

---

35 L. M. Montgomery, *Anne of Green Gables* (Puffin, 1908).

Weekly practices

How quickly do the weeks pass by? It's so easy for life to keep rolling on, merging and blending together, and before you know it, those weeks have collected into months. Weekly practices really help bring some punctuation into the rhythm of your life. Excuse me for pointing out the obvious, but there are fifty-two weeks in a year, so these practices come around often enough to really bring goodness, form and rhythm into your life.

Again, this isn't an exhaustive list of available weekly practices; there will also be space to add in your own. This, for me, is a list of things I do every week – I find my daily practices change with the seasons, but my weekly ones stay the same. This is because I need them to create stability and add form to my life. Consider your thoughts about them as you read. It's one of those tricky balances… we don't want to be rigid, but we do need consistency to produce the kind of spiritual life we want. This goes back to the science of habit formation that we discussed earlier.

Sabbath

Jon and I have practised a Sabbath for over ten years. Somehow we have managed to be consistent with it. I think that's because we *want* to do it. It is just so helpful! It's a relief to practise something that helps us remember regularly we are more than what we produce. I have come to believe that Sabbath is a day of rest or a day of delight. It is a day to just be and let our souls breathe, a day to reconnect more deeply with God and our own hearts, a day that is markedly different from the other six.

At the time of writing, our children are ten, twelve, fifteen and seventeen. Although we've kept the Sabbath over the last ten years, the way we have observed it has changed a lot! The kind of Sabbath that was realistic when we began ten years ago and our boys were one, three and five is totally different from today, and it has constantly been transforming over that time. There's definitely a lesson here: that although the practices can remain the same, their form can change as we do.

I think the key here is the essence of the day. In Exodus 20:8–10 it says, 'Remember the sabbath day by keeping it holy. Six days you shall labour and do all your work, but the seventh day is a sabbath to the Lord your God.' And in Mark 2:27, it says, 'The Sabbath was made for man, not man for the Sabbath.'[36]

In his book *Sabbath: The Ancient Practices*, Dan B. Allender says: 'The only parameter that is to guide our Sabbath is delight. Will this be merely a break or a joy? Will this lead my heart to wonder or routine? Will I be more grateful or just happy that I got something done?'[37]

We stick to a traditional twenty-four hours for our Sabbath. The time that works for us is Friday night at around 6 p.m. to Saturday night at around 6 p.m. Although the form and content have changed so much, we've kept the times the same over the whole last decade. We made this decision based on pure practicality, as neither of us work over these times. A lot of people choose to include a Sunday, but as leaders of a Christian community, Sunday is a working day for us. I would also strongly consider avoiding a Sunday if you are heavily involved in serving at church unless you experience that as restful and restorative. Sabbath increasingly feels less like a ritual to us and the kids, as it is now so natural and normal. They know

---

[36] Exodus 20:8–10 NIV; Mark 2:27 NIV.
[37] D. B. Allender, *Sabbath: The Ancient Practices* (Nashville, TN: Thomas Nelson, 2010), p. 47.

and we know that on Friday night whether things are done or not, we are having a break and we are having some fun.

The kids know Mum and Dad are fully present on this day. I think they exhale with us. I can see the ways that our older kids naturally incorporate this idea into their own lives now, even if it's not for spiritual reasons. They will make sure when they take on work shifts or study schedules for exams that they get a day off every week.

I'd love to show you how different it can look, so I'm going to share with you two examples of a Sabbath: one recent, and one from many years ago – my journalling practice is coming into its own here! I couldn't remember without it. I will name them like episodes from the sitcom *Friends*!

The one when the kids were young

When the kids were young, I found the days quite relentless and repetitive. Even though I enjoyed that season of parenting very much, I also struggled with the inevitable broken sleep that comes with caring for babies and toddlers. Jon worked full time in this season and was extremely hands-on when he was home. By the time it came to Sabbath, we were frankly exhausted! The main goal of Sabbath in this stage of our lives was rest. The boys were also too young to be deeply included in it, so we prioritised ourselves! I wince slightly as I type that, but I don't regret it, and I wouldn't change it, even if I had the chance to relive the season. It made us better parents; it made us kinder… we needed it! If you are in that season of life, can I encourage you, please don't waste a moment of your time on guilt for needing rest.

Practically, this meant we tried to eat food that we liked and was simple to prepare. Both of us are slightly introverted so we would batten down the hatches and spend the time together, just us. We gave each other two or three hours of solitude somewhere within the twenty-four-hour period while the other person took care of the kids. In that time, we did whatever we felt we needed to replenish our souls. A long walk, a swim, surfing, a bath, reading a book, taking a nap: things that often fall into the category of the non-classical practices we talked about earlier. Remember almost anything can be made sacred with the right heart posture, just like anything can be desecrated.

Then at some point in the day, we got out for a big walk all together. We packed hot chocolate or got ice creams while we were out, depending on the weather. We always got out of our town and went somewhere new. As both of us have a heart for adventure, this gave us a microdose we needed, and it broke the monotony of taking the same walks we always did the rest of the week. When time was more restricted, it was another way to say, 'this is a different day'.

You might notice I'm not mentioning much about specific prayer practices; this is because, for a long time, I've tried to live without a sacred/secular divide. It's all spiritual and prayerful if you lean your heart that way, so interwoven with and underpinning this day was and is always the fact that God is in and through all of it; I felt it then and I feel it now. Reading that book or taking that walk would always feel like an act of communion and union with God. St Basil the Great says it well: 'This is how you pray continually – not by offering prayer in words, but by joining yourself to God through your whole way of life, so that your life becomes one continuous and uninterrupted prayer.'[38]

As an avid multitasker, one of the things I like to do on Sabbath is to try to slow down and do one thing at a time. I like to be consciously unproductive and gloriously inefficient – like taking twenty minutes to slowly chop and arrange fruit for a snack, or to watch a film with my full attention, not scrolling through

---

38 Bishop K. Ware, *The Collected Works: Volume 1: The Inner Kingdom* (Crestwood, NY: St Vladimir's Seminary Press, 2000), p. 82, quoting 'Homily on the Martyr Julitta' 3–4.

Instagram at the same time. Not only does this help me to be more present, it also reminds me I am more than what I produce. It helps me embody being wholehearted and un-fragmented.

> Multitasking is the drive to be more than we are, to control more than we do, to extend our power and our effectiveness. Such practice yields a divided self, with full attention given to nothing.
> Walter Brueggemann[39]

I hope you take inspiration from this example of what a Sabbath can look like if you are in a particularly demanding or busy season of life. What one thing you can take away from this account?

The one that's completely ordinary

Sometimes we manage these epic Sabbaths where the house is perfect, no one argues, we reflect over what we are grateful for, and we can afford to eat out or go off on an adventure. But generally, they are very simple and beautifully imperfect.

Over the years, the kids have become more integrated into our Sabbath practice; we've been able to explain it and make it a nice experience for them as well – something to look forward to for all of us. It's also something that we prepare for, which they don't enjoy as much! One of the things I have learned is that I feel more rested if the house is tidy. That means that on Friday afternoons, there is often a decent effort at tidying the house. The kids moan of course, but I'm sure deep down they enjoy the feeling of getting it done – or maybe they really don't care! Sometimes we just don't have the time or the inclination to clean, and when that happens, so that we still feel that sense of rest, we normally just go out!

Remember Sabbath can't be taken only when all the work is

---

39 W. Brueggemann, *Sabbath as Resistance: Saying No to the Culture of Now* (Louisville, KN: Westminster John Knox Press, 2014), p. 67.

finished, or you will never manage to make it a weekly practice. Instead, it's knowing that we are resting now, whether things are finished or not, and that can be difficult for some. However, you soon learn the universe doesn't fall apart.

Typically, we get tidied up and have a nice meal that everyone likes, such as pizza or a fry-up. It's definitely not the time for broccoli soup in our house. That way, there's no moaning at dinner, because that is not a relaxing start for anyone. We then watch a movie or go for a walk somewhere different if we have the time. We no longer need to go off on our own very often because the kids are able to entertain themselves much more easily, and there aren't the demands and sleepless nights of those early years of parenting. The season of life is shifting again and sometimes our older teens aren't around, as they are out with friends. In this case, we try to just make sure about once a month that we get all of us together and go off for a picnic to somewhere beautiful like a loch or a mountain. It's no exaggeration to say that practising a Sabbath has really defined the last decade and the kids' upbringing. I think we are a stronger family because of our commitment to it, and because it has always included getting out into nature, our kids have learned to find rest, goodness, beauty and hopefully God there.

Building your own Sabbath

These are the kind of things you might want to consider when planning your Sabbath: What helps you to feel rested? What types of conversations are helpful for keeping you in the present moment? What kind of conversations drag you into stress or worry? This is not the time to chat about the instability of your mortgage rate or Uncle Edgar's drinking problem. Just the other day, Jon and I managed to grab an hour at the spa on our Sabbath while the kids were busy, and we were in the jacuzzi, a great place to relax… what could go wrong? But we found ourselves talking about money troubles. Jon said immediately, 'Let's not talk about this – it isn't a very Sabbath conversation.' This highlights that it isn't what you do or where you are, but your heart and intention that matters most. Anything can be experienced as stressful or restful. Remember you have everything you need to begin. Your ordinary life is enough.

However long you have practised, you will still need to be mindful. What brings you delight? What helps you feel close and connected to God? What restores your soul? Maybe a book by the fire? A walk in nature, a meal prepared and eaten slowly? Time with a friend? A chunk of silence? A long bath? A hard run?

What days and times are possible for you? Can you make it the same every week or does something like shift work mean you will have to be flexible with the time?

Do you want to give it a whole day, or do you want to start with a chunk of time? I would like to nail my colours to the mast here and say that unless you are in some sort of absolute crisis, no one should be working seven days a week. If you can, try for a whole day! There are exceptions of course, such as having substantial caring duties that are present every day. If so, is there a way to approach one day a week with a different heart posture? Or enlist a small bit of respite?

Another important thing is to consider your relationship with technology, particularly your phone. Do you want this to be a part of your Sabbath? Remember the Sabbath isn't just about resting; it's about delighting and trying to be present to your own heart, to God and your family and friends. Does your phone or TV help you to do that? I have been really up and down on this. Sometimes a great film speaks to my heart. But mindless scrolling on my phone definitely doesn't. I know in the main it doesn't help me to connect to the essence of Sabbath. My most common compromise is limited use or no social media on Sabbath. But just like all the examples in this book, it is not a set rule.

Review your week

The daily examen is a wonderful practice that we looked at extensively in the last section. Some of you may already have integrated it. Either way, I strongly recommend taking a bit more time weekly with a journal to do an extended version of the examen. You can use exactly the same prompts or any of your choosing, but also spend the time to go a bit deeper.

I practise this in community with The Prayer Orchard and members of our church online on a Sunday evening at 9 p.m. You are welcome to join us! I record the practice and other people catch up at a time that suits them better. It's a practice we do 'alone together'. It takes just fifteen minutes. We settle in with breathing and prayer, go through a version of the examen and then end by laying down the whole week at the feet of God, however we feel it has gone, whether things are finished or not. Then we receive the love of God by faith just as we are. Finally, we look ahead to the following week and consecrate it into God's hands.

The whole process helps to bring closure and acceptance to the week we are in and peace and direction for the week ahead. Just like all the practices explored in this book, it helps us to remember that God is with us and to abide. God is with us in the moments we remember and the ones we don't, the ones we are proud of and the ones we aren't, the light and the dark. There truly is nowhere we can go to escape the love or the presence of God. Ending every week remembering this is a wonderful, calming and formative practice.

Microdoses of silence, solitude and stillness

> We are starved for quiet, to hear the sound of sheer silence that is the presence of God himself.
> Ruth Haley Barton[40]

Microdoses of anything are difficult for me. I've had to work really hard at this practice to make sure I experience it as fruitful and not frustrating. Some of you will enjoy this kind of small interweaving. My natural personality is 'all or nothing'. There are times it's really good to work with your nature, and others when you just can't. It isn't possible for me to be a working mother of four and have everything my natural personality wants. I've had to learn that all or nothing isn't often an option for me.

These microdoses of, say, ten minutes to an hour might be something you integrate into your Sabbath, lunchtime walk or early morning. Whether you are a people person or not, we all need some time of solitude to just be on our own with God. We all need a time of stillness and silence to just be quiet and listen.

Think about a normal week in your life; is this something you already do? Or is it something you can see a way to schedule in? New practices often have to be intentionally integrated, and then they become second nature over time.

Prayer/talk with a soul friend

We need one another. Here in the West especially, we are in an increasingly individualistic society, and the results are in – it's not doing us any good. Jesus was around 'the many' sometimes, but on the whole, he was around 'the few' – his twelve disciples. Then

---

[40] R. H. Barton, *Invitation to Solitude and Silence: Experiencing God's transforming presence* (London: SPCK, 2021), p. 19.

he had the three – his inner circle. This is a really good relational model to draw inspiration from.

Other people see things differently, and they bring much needed insight and perspective into our lives. We all need people who we walk closely with and can trust deeply. In my experience, it isn't realistic to have a large number of friends we are this close to. Jesus' example of having an inner circle of three can be a helpful starting point.

I can count my close circle of friends on one hand. I meet with them regularly to talk, listen, pray, be honest, process, dream and lament, which enriches my life on every level. In some seasons of life, this occurs at a set time and place, and in some seasons, it has to be in grabbed moments when the opportunity arises. Obviously maintaining this as a rhythm can be hard because the more people involved, the harder it is to synchronise your diaries.

Although I didn't have this language back then, when our kids were young, I met up with two or three friends every week to pray. Sometimes we had our kids, sometimes we tried to meet when they were napping and over the years some of them were at school. I didn't live by a rule of life then; I hadn't even heard of one. But we all have habits, even if they aren't intentional. When I moved, this season naturally came to an end, and I haven't replaced it with an alternative in Scotland. Instead, new rhythms have emerged; they are different but they are equally as precious.

Is this something you feel that you already have in your life? Even if you don't describe it as I have? Or is there a friendship you could see has the potential to develop more depth in this way? This comes easy to some of us and can be hard for others. The internet is helpful here because if we are isolated or don't have any good friends nearby, we can at least catch up virtually. Which is such a gift… a real positive of technology!

Church/community gathering

> We go to church so as not to be alone – alone in our joys, alone in our suffering, alone in the everydayness of our lives, alone in the important passages of our lives... We go to church to tell people we love them, and hopefully, to hear them tell us the same thing.
> Ronald Rolheiser[41]

Church has been part of my faith journey from the very beginning. Anything you commit to in the long term has its ups and downs; it is simply the way things are. I have found deep friendship, learning, challenge, growth, hope, purpose and profound love in church. I have had seasons over the last twenty years when I could have easily just walked out, never to return, especially when I was wrestling deeply with my theological beliefs. I have also had times when I haven't found it especially rewarding or life-giving. I've been hurt by people, I've been bored, I've been disillusioned, I'd even go as far to say that I have experienced spiritual trauma as a result of certain things I was taught. However, despite this, for me it has been right to remain within a church, and my relationship with God and continued spiritual development have been the fruits of that choice.

I know for some people, for a massive variety of reasons, church might not be right for you in this season of life – especially if there has been trauma involved. If you *are* in a church and you've just been dragging yourself there even though it's no longer spiritually nourishing, it might be time for a new one. There is a season for everything under heaven... a time to dig deep and stick it out, but also a time to leave! If you need permission to explore, consider it fully granted! If you have experienced trauma due to church in one way or another, there are excellent resources available and people

---

41 R. Rolheiser, *Holy Longing: The Search for a Christian Spirituality* (New York: Doubleday, 1999), p. 134.

who specialise in helping people heal from this. I have referenced them at the back of the book. There is no part of me that is saying church is something everybody has to be a part of. I do, however, think there is so much wisdom and benefit to engaging in some form of regular Christian community.

If this is you, are there other Christians you can gather with to pray, learn and share food with? There are many wonderful expressions of Christian community around these days. I encourage you to explore prayerfully and see what you can find.

What does Christian community look like for you currently? What are your hopes and desires for it? Are there any changes that you feel invited to? Or a healing journey that could be embarked upon?

Mid-week house group/hobby/prayer group

Many people attend a group on a weekly basis with others. This helps to deepen your spiritual experience. This might be something obvious like a mid-week Bible study or prayer group, or it could be something less obvious, like a sport or eco-group or anything that helps you feel connected to God and others. Don't discount anything. If it works for you, then it can become a spiritual practice. What do you already do? Is there space for something to be added in here? If so, what things could fit this category for you?

Time in nature

I have had the privilege of living near the sea for the past twenty-two years; fourteen in Cornwall in the south-west of England and eight in East Lothian on the east coast of Scotland. Even with easy access to the beach, woodland and countryside, I still have to make a choice to enter nature. I have to choose to enter it with my body, but also with my mind and heart. Quite often, if I'm doing an ordinary task that happens in nature, my body is there but my mind can be busy with worries and to-do lists. Taking some time once a week to immerse myself in nature and be fully present is a gift to my soul. Even surrounded by beauty, I need to be intentional to soak it in.

Activity

Prayerfully read Wendell Berry's poem 'The Peace of Wild Things'.[42] Do you access nature on a regular basis? Do you feel a desire to? Are there barriers to this for you?

Review of weekly practices

These are the weekly practices that I have built by trial and error over time. As you have now read this section, ask yourself these questions: What have you noticed? Do you already do any of these things? Do you feel drawn to include any of them into your own weekly practices? Are there any other intentional practices you can think of that you would like to try to include? What are the times, or lengths of time that seem fitting for you as you consider what a week looks like for you? Does your week follow a similar kind of pattern, or is there a lot of variability? These will be important things to consider as you discern the path ahead.

---

42 W. Berry, *The Peace of Wild Things: And Other Poems* (London: Penguin, 2018), p. 25.

Monthly practices

Sorry for stating the obvious again, but when it comes to monthly practices, we have twelve per year, or three per season. Unlike weekly practices, these are infrequent enough to need to get something in the diary. There is flexibility for the dates within the month to change quite a lot. These practices are also going to be unique to you, to your personality, your capacity and the general season of life you are in. So, bring your full imagination to this chapter!

My husband and I have been married for nineteen years, and we've been parents seventeen of them. As a person who is married and a mother, when I am planning my practices, I don't just have myself to consider – it has to work for my family, too. What circumstances do you have to consider? What are your time limitations and parameters? Is your capacity limited in other ways? Maybe you have a very demanding job or ill health, or you look after a family member?

Your circumstances never exclude you from building a rule of life, but I think it's fair to say it isn't easy for everyone, and some people need a little more imagination and creativity than others to put things in place.

For us, just like I described in the Sabbath practice, there has been a lot of give and take over the years as working parents of a large family. We love to do things together when we can manage it. But we have also released each other so much over the years, and this has built into an important monthly practice of giving each other the space to do something that feeds our soul. We haven't been as consistent with this as with the weekly practices. However, we've done our best. Here are our monthly practices.

A time of silence, solitude and stillness

If you picked this book up off the shelf, then you have some interest in deepening your spirituality and your sense of connection to God. That can feel like a vague esoteric concept. What does it even mean to connect to God? In that desire, we are naming our need for a deeper connection formed in faith. We want to deepen our awareness of the unseen, unprovable, supernaturally divine. It means that, amid cooking dinner, checking email and worrying about the state of the economy, we want to live for and be aware of God. We want to be aware of the reality that we are always immersed in the Divine Presence and part of something much larger than our own lives.

I can't speak for your life, but my everyday doesn't scream supernatural divinity at first glance. I have to LOOK FOR IT, SEEK IT, PRIORITISE IT, SURRENDER TO IT, WRESTLE FOR IT. It doesn't just happen. Just as it never does for anyone.

Even the lives we have explored of the mystics and saints are full of doubt, struggles and hardships. They too had times when heaven felt silent, and they experienced long dark nights of the soul.

The little bits of silence, solitude and stillness that we cultivate in our daily and weekly practices add up and make a difference. But to pop something longer in monthly can be amazingly fruitful. And hey, this is about doing the best you can with what you have. The best amount of time is the amount of time you can manage, whether that's a day/half day or just a couple of hours. In our noisy/busy/distracting world, it is so beneficial to our spiritual life that I would go as far to say that it is essential to carve out this time. In any relationship there is both talking and listening. This gives us another way to listen to God, to create spaciousness.

> Spaciousness is always a beginning, a possibility, a potential, a capacity for birth.
> Gerald May.[43]

Silence, solitude and stillness often come together, but I would like to separate them out and say a few things about each of the practices separately.

Silence

> I'm praying, I'm saying nothing to him, I'm just loving him.
> St Thérèse of Lisieux[44]

I am a self-confessed chatterbox; however, as I have got older and incorporated silence as a practice, it has slowly but surely made itself my friend. In fact, when I step into silence now, that's exactly how I experience it. It really is like greeting a friend. I have come to believe that the friend I am meeting as I enter silence is both God and my own deepest, truest self. It's like they finally have a chance to say hello to each other. Maybe they are always saying hello to each other, I'm not sure; maybe it's that I am finally quiet enough to notice and consciously join the party.

Silence is not just the absence of noise but the endless expanse of possibility. There are two types of silence: interior and exterior. Interior silence is formed and experienced from consistent practice of exterior silence. I am not blessed with a disposition that leans towards either of these, but with practice I am getting better!

Exterior silence

This is the bit we can cultivate and practice: being silent, not speaking, humming, singing or making any noise. It's also having

---

43 G. G. May, *The Awakened Heart: Opening Yourself to the Love You Need* (Harper SanFrancisco, 2009), p. 106.

44 J. Udris and L. Muir, *The Gift of Thérèse of Lisieux* (Leominster, Herefordshire: Gracewing, 2009), p. 61.

the least input possible to your circumstances, so no music or podcasts. Sounds of things like traffic or nature are, of course, unavoidable in most circumstances. A regular practice of exterior silence leads to varying degrees and experiences of interior silence. Are you ever intentionally and prayerfully silent? Are you drawn to it, or not? Would you consider integrating this as a monthly practice?

Interior silence

This is an inner state of just being. It is just being with God and your own heart at peace. It's often fleeting because as soon as you notice 'Hey, I'm not thinking about anything!' it's already over. But the moments are beautiful when they come, and they nourish your spirit in a way little else does. It's like a deeply satisfying drink of water for the soul. A little glimpse of union, where you get to just exist briefly in that union with God without worry or analysis of any kind.

My experiences of these moments have been few and far between as I naturally have an extremely busy mind. I try to accept that with as much grace as I can. The plus side is that it is even more precious when it does happen.

Silence can be shared, but this can be difficult if you are aiming for longer periods of time, and obviously doesn't work at all if you are combining it with solitude!

To get started, you can decide if you would rather be inside or outside, at home or away from home. I find home a tricky place to practise silence because, even alone in my house, it's easy to be distracted by all the things I need to do. If there is anyone else in the house, then just forget it. The only time it would work for me to be silent in my house would be alone in the bath or on a Sabbath when the house has just been cleaned and everyone else has vanished. To have all those puzzle pieces fall into place is extremely rare so I normally just go out! Again, this is a way of working with my reality rather than against it; it saves me so much frustration.

I am blessed to have three sacred, special indoor places to go to for times of silence. One is a shepherd's hut owned by a family who are special friends of ours. Its sole purpose is to provide a place of spiritual refuge, where people can encounter the Good Shepherd. Second is a remote woodland cabin owned by another family in our community. Both of these places are less than half an hour away from our home. Third is a Christian retreat centre that is about a ninety-minute drive away. This is more expensive and needs an entire day, so it makes up one or two of my monthly times a year, but I absolutely love it when I get to go. It's called The Bield at Blackruthven and it's in Perth in Scotland. You should visit if you ever get the chance. You can wear a wee badge saying 'I am in silence' and then no one talks to you. I thought about trying to wear the badge at home… I don't think it would work!

When I am not able to get to one of these amazing places, I head out into nature. I am blessed to live in a place where safe, accessible, solitary nature is close by. I get there with ease, but with a little imagination, you can find pockets of nature in urban areas like parks or small woodlands.

Silence seemed daunting to me at first. Would I be bored? When I stop talking, would the internal noise increase? What exactly would I discover? Silence can be very exposing. If it isn't a regular practice for you, then start small and build it up. If you have a friend who is keen, you really can practise together. You can also choose what you want to do in your silence: be in nature, dance, walk, do a craft, create, paint, bake, write – your imagination is your only limit. It can be an incredible time to connect with a loved one. My husband was once attending a silent retreat day I was leading. After I had done the opening session and sounded the gong for silence, he wanted to communicate to me that I had done a great job. Without being able to use words, he touched my arm to get my attention, looked at me deeply with teary eyes, pointed at me and made prayer hands and smiled. So much love and connection was transmitted between us in that moment. It's such a noisy world that it can be a relief to just be quiet sometimes.

I guess the other really important thing to address is, what's the point of being silent? In my experience, silence creates space. It creates a space for connection to be birthed. A space to listen. A space for things to come up. A space that feels different from other parts of our lives. A space to ponder or just to be more present to what *is*. It's a spiritual practice found in many traditions. As we shrink our outer world in this way, our inner world has the chance to grow. We contract this one thing and invite expansion on so many other levels.

How do you feel about silence? What are your current experiences of it? Can you see a way of incorporating it monthly? What could it look like for you? Are you more drawn to practising alone or with a friend?

Solitude

Become your own best friend.
Cory Muscara[45]

We are living in an age of hyper connectivity and yet an increasing lack of deep, meaningful connection. It is an age of social media likes and projecting an image. It's incredibly important to know who we are outside of our connection to others and their opinions. We need to be alone at times to experience the deepest, richest and most real relationship we can ever have – that with our creator. There are seasons in life where this is near to or completely impossible; I will address these later in the book. But for most of us, getting some solitude is possible, and if it's something that isn't available to you on a daily or weekly basis, then I would highly recommend trying to make the time for some solitude on a monthly basis. This

---

[45] Cory Muscara, Instagram post, 16 April 2024: https://www.instagram.com/reel/C50xlZcLRhu/ (accessed 20 January 2025).

could be time alone in the house, on a walk, in the bath, or during a movement practice.

Solitary activities can be deeply connecting, like going alone to a library or a cafe even if you aren't completely alone as there are other people around. For those of you who live alone or work a solitary job, this might be something you experience often in everyday life. But is there a way of incorporating intentional times of solitude with an opportunity to connect with God? Are you drawn to solitude or resistant to it? Why? Is this something you already practise or would like to begin?

Stillness

Stillness is fundamentally the ceasing of activity. It is a time of being physically still, with the hopes that you will also become internally still, much like with silence. This is probably the hardest one for me to integrate into my life. The only time I practise it is when I'm in centering prayer. I'm not sure of 'the rules' but I don't think sitting on the sofa and watching Netflix counts, which is a shame as otherwise I would have this one totally nailed! Are you ever still? Why or why not?

Within your monthly practices you can decide if you want to integrate just one of silence, solitude and stillness or combine a couple. A silent walk alone is a great example, and is silence and solitude. Sitting by a river and just watching it flow by could combine all three. Doing a prayerful painting in silence with a friend could just be the silence. It's totally up to you. But something from this category planned in the diary once a month will bear fruit for you. It's just a case of choosing something and getting started.

Spiritual direction

We are spiritual companions. We are the holders of stories, keepers of secrets, guides for the silent lands. We nurture safe

spaces, protect the pauses, listen for what words cannot say. We are companions not leaders who come carrying candles, not maps. We notice, we name, we help you seek just the next step. We ask our questions gently, mirror your words lovingly, offer our practices playfully. We welcome the tears, the laughter, the swears. We trust in the slow unfolding of things.
Jen Goodyer[46]

Until about six years ago, I had never heard of a spiritual director. I think it depends on the Christian tradition you find yourself in. Now I am one and I'm surrounded by them, and most people in my community see one. They are available online or in person. Monthly is a good frequency to see a spiritual director; it's often enough that they are part of the flow of your life. Some are expensive, some are donation based. Most want to be accessible to everyone regardless of finances. I wouldn't consider not having a spiritual director now. It's an absolute priority for me. My spiritual director is the person I can be entirely vulnerable with. She has helped me wrestle and find clarity through some of the hardest situations of my life.

Spiritual directors differ from receiving pastoral advice or seeing a therapist. The name 'director' can be deceiving; they aren't like a directive coach. They are more like a spiritual companion, helping to illuminate the path you are already walking on with God. When Jen Goodyer describes them as carrying a candle not a map, that hits the nail on the head for me. I have seen three different spiritual directors over the last three years for different reasons. One was in person at a retreat centre several times a year until she retired. My current director, who I meet with online, is a somatic spiritual director and helps me get to the root of things in my life. I have also spent the last year meeting weekly with a spiritual director

---

46 Jen Goodyer, Instagram post, 21 September 2023: https://www.instagram.com/p/Cxc6onxM-8K (accessed 20 January 2025).

who is guiding me through the Ignatian Spiritual Exercises. All of these women have had a profound effect on my spiritual journey. They provide a place I can come to; be totally myself, not be judged; be held, find hope and discern how God might be moving and speaking in my life. Seeing a spiritual director is a high priority for anyone who is interested in deepening their spiritual lives.

Do you see a spiritual director? Would you like to?

Soul friend

I have placed this in both the weekly and monthly section to give options of form and frequency. It may be that your soul friend lives nearby or you're in the same church, so you naturally catch up every week. But once a month, you decide to have a dedicated meet up. Or it may be that you live far away from each other and a monthly catch up on the phone/Zoom is what you both have capacity for. Our lives are all so different. There is no right or wrong way to do things. Again, there is another person/people involved here too, so you have them to consider as well when making plans.

Soul friends differ from spiritual directors because the relationship is mutual; you are supporting each other. A spiritual director may become your friend, but it remains a professional relationship; certainly within the sessions themselves there are professional boundaries. Who are the friends you already have who are like soul friends? Is there a potential friendship/connection that could deepen in this way?

The examen

You may be surprised to see this practice come up again. I know it may seem repetitive, but repetition is good in spiritual practice; think back to the monasteries with their prayer five times a day. Consider if a monthly examen-style review could be another helpful rhythm to bring into your life. The things that come up for you within the practice could then be integrated into some of the other practices we have discussed in this section. For example, it could help you distil your thoughts before meeting with your soul friend or spiritual director. It may be that you choose the examen daily and monthly but you don't do it weekly; again, it is about finding the rhythm that works for you. Is this something you can see benefit from incorporating monthly?

Seasonal practices

As people of a Christian faith, we believe in God as the creator and source of all things. It doesn't matter at all whether you believe in a literal creation story, the Big Bang or something else. I've never met any Christian who doesn't believe God is somehow involved in or the source of creation.

Works of art tell us a story. They aren't the creator in themselves, but they reflect their creators. The world has so much to teach us about the nature of God. It isn't just for information about the character and beauty of the Trinity, although of course we get the gift of that, too. The rhythms of the seasons and the natural world can also teach us wisdom on how to live. These things are not just found in nature; they are also reflected in how our bodies are created: the natural limits of our humanity, the boundaries that help us to flourish. The natural has so much to teach us about the spiritual, and that's because the source of the natural is spiritual! The source of you is God. The source of nature is God. It's the invisible mystery made partially visible. The more we look, the more we see.

Historically, we couldn't ignore nature like we can now. We worked when it was light, ate what was in season and were much more connected to the land. There are people both within and outside of the Church who have very little connection with or appreciation for the natural world. Progress is wonderful, and, as a resident in Scotland, I love central heating! But there is always a hidden cost. We aren't necessarily better off because of the progress we've made. How many people do you know who are always exhausted and pushing their limits? You could be reading that thinking it sounds like you. I know several people who struggle to enjoy their annual leave, because every time they completely rest, their body shuts down or they become ill. That's a sure sign you're doing too much.

Electric light and non-stop connection to work emails don't honour our limits. They mean we need to put boundaries in to honour them ourselves. I'm always happy when I email someone and get that automatic out-of-office reply. And it always disturbs me when I email/message someone about something and I get a reply at 2 a.m.… Please don't worry about my email at 2 a.m. – go to sleep!

It is really important when developing a rule of life to have practices that you stick to; it makes it so much easier to foster discipline. Leaning on an example found in nature, did you know we tend to digest our food better if we eat at roughly the same time each day? We do want to have certain elements of our rule that don't change, to bring stability, but keeping everything exactly the same all year round actually ends up going against the natural order of things. Your energy levels in midsummer probably won't be the same as your energy levels in deep winter, and nor should they be. The more we awaken to and work with nature, the more we realise how wonderful it is. I can't believe, for example, that I used to think I needed exactly the same amount of sleep in June as I do in December. I don't! It's such a relief to give myself a bit more sleep in the darker months and enjoy a few more late nights in the summer. My energy levels benefit from it. I think that even some of the monasteries kept a different prayer schedule in summer from the one they did in winter.

How do we keep the routine and discipline that we learn from our monastic forefathers and mothers, but flex and flow with the natural seasons within the calendar year? What should we keep the same and what should we adapt?

Is it exactly the same for men as it is for women? St Francis talked about Brother Sun and Sister Moon. I have no idea what they knew about hormone cycles back when St Francis lived, but a lot of the ancient wisdom literature also links the feminine to the moon and the masculine to the sun. Science has now proven what ancient people knew instinctively. We know that men run on a twenty-four-hour hormone cycle like the daily rising and setting of the sun, and women (for their menstruating years at least) run on a roughly twenty-nine-day cycle just like the moon, with several hormones waxing and waning over that time.

I'm generalising here and, of course, there are exceptions, but men tend to be much better with a routine that stays the same every day like their hormone cycle, while women tend to be better with more flexibility over the month like their hormone cycle. There's a large amount of information on this topic so do look it up online if you're interested in exploring it further.

How do we start working with ourselves and our natural rhythms, rather than against? This is a big question with many facets. It could get overwhelming, so choose to not let it and we'll keep it simple. If we are going to live in line with the natural order of things, we are going to slow down enough to stop and smell the roses! The spiritual life is not a rushed one. I'll say it again: the spiritual life is not a rushed one.

There is no skipping the process; there are no microwaves to get spiritual maturity in five minutes. We are going to have to practise paying attention and having regular times of reflection to live lives that honour our limits and the season we are in, natural, spiritual or otherwise. The reflective practices that we discussed, such as the examen, really help us here. We are going to need to go outside into nature regularly so we can see the trees bud, blossom and drop their leaves, reminding us that we aren't meant to bloom all year round either. We are going to need to get off the merry-go-round of our culture's non-stop, 24/7 way of doing things. All things at all times is *not* what is best for us. We are created to wax and wane, to fast and feast, to work and play, to produce and rest. Those of you who are very driven and for whom the thought of slowing down or – even worse – stopping makes you sweat, don't worry. I'll throw you a bone here – living this way actually boosts productivity.

Once we've grasped that we are going to need to live at a sustainable pace, the next task is to take time quarterly to do a seasonal view. This is a wonderful practice that can be integrated into your rule of life.

A seasonal review

A seasonal review of your 'rule' is a fruitful thing to do. You could either pick your own dates that land roughly before the turn of the seasons or, if you want to choose some that already exist, you could go for the summer and winter solstice and the spring and autumn equinox, although these are mid-season. Don't feel bound by the milestones that the culture associates with change. For example, new year's resolutions happen smack bang in the middle of winter, which nature tells us isn't the time try to bring energy into making changes. Look at the trees; they are still deepening their roots and resting, not bearing new life. That's spring's job.

At every turn of season, I invite you to develop a practice of reviewing your rule and doing a general life pause and reset. This can be integrated with any amount of time and depth that you have available to you, depending on your wider context at the time. Got a newborn or a dissertation to get in? Maybe all you do to mark the change of season is to look out the window and ponder the changing leaves on the trees! But most of us can go a bit deeper. There are two main ways to look at it.

The four seasons

> It was you who set all the boundaries of the earth; you made both summer and winter.
> Psalm 74:17 NIV

We've already mentioned the natural seasons, but I have a few specific thoughts I'd like to share about them. Please feel free to adapt them or add your own. It's good to acknowledge our preferences and how we experience the seasons. This isn't always obvious. At first glance, I would have always said I'm a 'summer person'. I love the heat and the increased light and the beach and the holidays. But actually, when I reflect deeper, I can really struggle in the summer because I burn myself out. I don't sleep as well. I overplan. I become frazzled and literally and figuratively overheated. Even though I'm less drawn to it on the surface, I flourish more in the winter. It cools and calms my natural personality, giving me time to breathe. I thrive on the quietness of it. It balances out all my natural fire. I've only noticed this very recently as I have begun to live at a pace that makes me capable of noticing such things. In summer, I wonder if I get lost in the endless nature of the possibilities. As you read through the next section, have these questions in mind: Which season are you most drawn to? Which season do you resist the most? Why? St Ignatius taught that both our consolations, which draw us nearer to God, and desolations, which lead us away from God, teach us and that we should pay attention to both. It's helpful to bear these in mind if you decide to do a seasonal review of your spiritual practices, as it may help you discern and make choices.

Winter

The days are colder, darker and shorter. It's likely that you'll have reduced energy levels and an increased need for sleep. It's the season of warm, hearty, nourishing foods like soups and stews.

This is a time for rest, withdrawal and deepening. Think of trees without leaves deepening their roots and resting from sustaining fruit. Think of bears hibernating. It's OK for you to have reduced productivity. Instead, embrace quietness, solitude, reading, fires and stargazing.

Spring

The days are warmer and lighter. You may have more energy in this season and higher productivity. It's the season for lighter, fresher foods such as spring greens and cooked vegetables and grains.

This is a time for awakening and the possibility of new life. Think of budding trees potent with new beginnings, and daffodils. It's the reintroduction of colour and blossoming connections.

Summer

The plants are now fully in bloom, and the longer, hotter days make summer a time for connection and adventure. You're more likely to feel energetic and productive and have a reduced need for sleep. This is the season for raw foods like fruit and seasonal salads.

This is a time to connect. Think of full, ripe nature and trees heavy with leaves and fruit.

Autumn

The cooler, darkening and shortening days of autumn may mean you have reduced energy levels. This is a season for cooked, slightly heavier foods like mushrooms and root vegetables.

It is a time for a slow drawing away and inward. It is a time for shedding, releasing and letting go. Think of autumn leaves on trees changing colour and falling to the ground.

A note for menstruating women: the outer seasons can be applied to the inner seasons of your cycle – winter represents our bleed, spring is the build-up to ovulation, summer is your ovulation and autumn is the build-up to your bleed. I use this rhythm to help me plan the optional things within my control each month. It's another way to work with my God-given nature and it's been a game changer for me.

Pulling it together

You may be thinking that all of this sounds great if we lived in the olden days, are retired with no responsibilities or in some sort of fairytale just dancing around with birds. But what about the rest of us juggling nine-to-five jobs, families or financial stress with very little flexibility or control over how our seasons are mapped out?

We have to look for small ways to integrate the seasons. I'm self-employed so some aspects of my work I can adapt, but the bulk is the same every week, all year round. I imagine there are very few of us who can have total freedom to plan our lives exactly as we want, but you may have more flexibility than you think. Here is a list of a few small things you could do to adapt to each season. Please let this spark your creativity so you can come up with your own ideas to add to it.

All seasons
- Go outside into nature, observe and pray. What is your one takeaway?
- Do an inner and outer cleanse of some type
- Review your rule of life
- Eat one extra, local in-season food

Winter
- Go to bed slightly earlier
- Say no to something social
- Include an extra reflective/solitude practice in your rule of life
- Drink warm drinks
- Find a quiet, solitary project
- Think ahead to optional commitments and make sure you have the energy to expend on them

Spring
- Observe some sunrises/sunsets
- Notice the lengthening day
- Say yes to something social

- Is there anything you sense you want to begin, any new life budding through after the deepening of winter?

Summer
- Go to bed later or get up a bit earlier
- Enjoy, play, create!
- Complete a project
- Socialise

Autumn
- Observe some sunrises/sunsets
- Notice the shortening day and remind yourself that no one can be or should be at maximum capacity all the time
- Can you reduce one thing you do in some way, to reflect the waning energy of nature?
- Is there anything you are being invited to let go of like the trees shedding their leaves?

Whatever the natural season is now as you are reading, is there something you can do from the list? Are there things you already adapt instinctively according to the seasons?

Here is an example of how I adapt some elements of my rule of life according to the seasons.

Winter	Spring	Summer	Autumn
Wake at 6 a.m.	Wake at 5:15 a.m.	Wake at 5:15 a.m. or earlier if I had an early night	Wake at 5:45 a.m.

Winter	Spring	Summer	Autumn
Go to bed by 10 p.m. latest if I can	Go to bed before 10:30 p.m.	Go to bed before 11 p.m.	Go to bed before 10:30 p.m.
Increase solitude and silence	Extra community prayer practice	Plan to attend a Christian festival if possible	Increase solitude and silence
2 × 20 mins centering prayer a day	20 mins centering prayer a day	20 mins centering prayer a day	20 mins centering prayer a day
Morning practices inside	A couple of times a week do morning practices outside	Do morning practices outside as much as I can	A couple of times a week do morning practices outside
Try to go out and look at the stars	Try to catch a sunrise or sunset	Go and watch the moon rise over the ocean	Try to catch a sunrise or sunset

Inner and outer cleanses

A set time that could involve a fast or a cleanse could be a great way to mark every season. It can then be used as a launchpad to review your rule of life. Has anything changed in your work or relationships? Are there different practices you feel led to or away from because of the change of season? For example, I find that in the winter when it's dark I always do my morning practices inside, but when it's summer I like to go out some of the time. As I'm in a marriage with someone else who also likes to get outside early, we need to have a chat and make a plan that works for both of us. All this sort of thing prevents life just happening to us and reduces little offences or missed opportunities because of a lack of foresight or poor communication.

Outer seasonal clean

This is an opportunity to look at and look after your space. This could be your home, bedroom, office or garden. It's an opportunity to remember once again that everything is spiritual. The concrete ordinary practices such as cleaning may not be obviously spiritual but are places where we can meet God if we choose to open our eyes. There is no sacred/secular divide except the one we create. God is in and through all things. Even if you are a person who keeps on top of everything – which I am not! – it's always good to set aside time for those deeper cleaning jobs. Our environment affects our energy and mood, and who has the time or inclination to deep clean all the time? The very act of pulling things out and cleaning behind them, sorting paperwork and belongings is physical, but it often produces a spiritual mirroring.

Even if you can afford a cleaner or someone else does the cleaning in your home, I encourage you to do the deep clean yourself if you are physically able. The process, not just the end results, are so critical to obtaining the transformation that is available. If we are open, it's a natural time for thoughts to come up about what else we might want to clear out, like negative thought patterns or un-forgiveness. Maybe the cleanliness in the physical space ignites desire to clean up or sort out habits that have crept into your lives. It's the classic effect of pulling on a thread – you sort one area, and the desire grows to sort others. You see the dirt and dust behind your desk, and you suddenly become more aware of the 'dirt and dust' gathering in an area of your work or relationships. Never underestimate the power of simple, practical tasks to yield profound spiritual fruit. It's all connected, or as the saying goes: 'How we do anything is how we do everything.'[47]

There can be little rituals that mark a new season, such as packing away the blankets after winter or buying a candle that has a new scent reflecting the new season. I adjust the colour I paint my toenails to the season. As I write, it's winter so they are a deep, dark green. It isn't the time for coral. These little things can help us feel more connected to the natural world when often our jobs or modern lifestyles prevent us. The more aware we are, the more present we will be to the lessons interwoven in the natural world as it reflects and points to its creator.

Physical and spiritual clean/cleanse/fast

Dirt and grime build up in unseen places in our homes, and the same happens in our spiritual lives and our bodies. Some form of physical cleansing is present across most of the religions and traditions in the world. It helps our physical bodies function better and gives them time to heal. Unprocessed, un-dealt-with spiritual problems have a chance to come up during these times of cleansing. You will begin to notice the cumulative aspect of these practices. Your first deep physical cleanse might be pretty awful – it can be a report card on how you've been living – but the more you practise, and the healthier your system is, the less confronting the detox symptoms will be. This is exactly the same spiritually; the more you deal with un-forgiveness, habits and resentments, the fewer there are to deal with.

Your theology on fasting is going to be important here. Why are you actually doing it? What do you think it will achieve? Do you believe fasting moves the hand of God? That it helps your prayers be heard? Do you believe it transforms you? It's good to consider what

---

47 This quote is most commonly attributed to Martha Beck.

you've been taught and what you actually believe. You could talk to others and explore it.

Regularly fasting or cleansing helps us to keep in touch with our bodies and attend to our health. We humans can, on the whole, do a pretty poor job at respecting the body. We follow a God who loves creation so much that Christ actually put on flesh and became human. However hard you try to spiritualise everything, you can't bypass the body. Doing a cleanse seasonally can help you to observe how your body's needs change over time. Again, a lot of us are so busy and disconnected that we don't take the time to notice our body until it is screaming at us through an illness or similar. Even then, we often just want to get past it.

If you have a history of eating disorders, please don't consider any kind of fasting that involves food. Stick with the tech fast or another non-food-related type of restriction.

I have a liver condition that means I can't do any fasting that involves total abstinence from food; even juice cleanses would be problematic to me. As a result, I focus on other cleanses that don't involve completely cutting out food.

There are also a few different common types of fasting that we can explore below.

Fasting from food

This involves abstaining from all food but drinking water. There are lots of references to this type of fasting within the Bible. The premise is that the discomfort of withholding food prompts you to turn towards deeper spiritual nourishment. If you want to take part in this sort of fasting, I advise treating the body with kindness and easing in and out of it with thoughtfulness. Heavily reducing things like wheat, caffeine and sugar in the build-up means you are less likely to experience withdrawal from those things. This would become a distraction in itself during the fast. It's not very loving to have a Big Mac and Coke the night before and then stop eating and expect spiritual transformation the next day! We want to work with the body and not against it. Unfortunately, the ignoring and disrespecting of our body within spirituality is something I see in the Church all the time. It's good to ease back into eating, breaking the fast with care and eating simple foods. Stewed apples with a little cinnamon is one of the best 'breaking a fast' foods.

Daniel fast

The Daniel fast is a partial fast based on a story from the biblical book of Daniel and drawn from chapter ten, verse three: 'I ate no choice food; no meat or wine touched my lips; and I used no lotions at all until the three weeks were over.'[48] It's a strict vegan diet that prohibits animal products, leavened breads, processed foods, caffeine and alcohol for between ten and twenty-one days. This is a good option if you don't want to or can't totally fast. This will have a mild detox effect on the body, so on a practical note, remember that if you normally don't eat much vegetarian food such as lentils and beans, you might also want to introduce some slowly before the fast or you are going to end up being pretty gassy and uncomfortable! It's about wisdom and kindness to your body.

Tech fast

This is probably becoming more and more relevant in our technology-obsessed society. I often put boundaries around my tech when I'm fasting to create even more time, space and the ability to listen to God. But it is brilliant as a stand-alone fast. It reduces so much noise and distraction, especially if you are in a period of discernment. It's great in a time of silence, solitude and stillness.

---

48 Daniel 10:3 NIV.

The church calendar

Those in churches that use more liturgy have the gift of being well integrated with the church calendar already. But those of us who aren't in those churches can be far less familiar with it. It can be incredibly grounding to follow patterns and repetition, particularly when so much around us swirls and changes. Much like the natural seasons, although they are always in flux, it's reassuring to know that winter will follow autumn, and summer will follow spring – although it's not always that obvious in the temperature if you're in the UK! It's the same with the church calendar, which observes key times such as Advent and Lent, feast and saint days, Pentecost and Epiphany. These dates provide us with a grounding and keep us swept up into the larger narrative of Scripture and the kingdom. They keep us connected to one another, and to those who have gone before us and paved the way.

One way of integrating this into your rule of life is to look ahead at what is coming up in the church calendar. You can find simple ways to include it in your practices. For example, are there any saints' feast days coming up? Maybe that day you could take a pause from some of your usual practices and do something that helps you mark the occasion, like reading something they have written or doing an act of kindness inspired by them. If it's St Francis of Assisi, you could do something to care for nature that day. If it's Julian of Norwich, you could spend a little longer in 'your cell' or offer a listening ear to a friend. This is so beautiful because it connects us more deeply with the lineage of our faith. It keeps it alive and fresh, fluid and active. It helps make your faith feel like something you are living and embodying in the midst of the ordinary.

Annual practices

I love Christmas: the pretty lights, the presents, the feasting, the gift-giving. But even as much as I love it, I'm glad it only comes around once a year. The same goes for my birthday and the birthdays of those I love. Special events like these require saving and planning. They require effort and energy, and wonderful as they are, we wouldn't want or be able to celebrate these annual events more frequently.

The three practices I am outlining in this section are much the same. They are special and important. They require investment, energy and planning. They are things that, for most of us, are only realistic and appropriate to do once a year or even every couple of years. I want to put in a little word of caution here and encourage you to consider planning these things in, just like all of the other practices. If anything, I wonder if they're more important to plan. We expect the weeks and the months to roll on by, but years seem so sparse that we think they won't. But they do. It's easy to let years pass by, so even though these are infrequent, they can fall into a 'later' category that never comes.

The three yearly practices I am outlining are: retreat, pilgrimage and mission. At first glance there might be some blurred lines, but these are three very distinct practices, with different histories and intentions behind them. They each form a unique part of our spiritual experiences and are all valuable. You could do some sort of expression of all of them every year if that's possible for you, but you certainly don't have to.

As you have journeyed with me through this book, my hope is that you have felt included, equipped and able to participate in some way in some of the practices. I don't expect that any reader will have wanted to partake in all of them – that would be a bit overkill! The annual practices, I think, can feel the most challenging to approach and to incorporate. I know as a working mum of four, I have certainly felt that way. A month's pilgrimage to the Holy Land, overseas mission trips or long retreats at fancy centres definitely haven't been in reach for me in the main. But that is not the point, and as we have learned from observing the life of Jesus and other saints and monks, spiritual practice is about less, not more. It's about stripping back to see who we will become, not about what we have or what we do. Our intention to be with and love God is most important. It's not about doing it perfectly.

The commercialisation of spirituality is a big and tricky subject, but there is a time and place for things to cost money. I think it's fair that we pay for people's skills and resources. That said, a lack of finances should never be seen as a barrier to knowing or loving God. Trust me, you can meet God as you are, with what you have, in any season of your life.

Over the years, I have learned to incorporate the essence of these practices with my capacity and circumstances. I am pleased to let you know there are ways to personalise and adapt these three spiritually enriching yearly practices into your life, too.

Retreat

> Then, because so many people were coming and going that they did not even have a chance to eat, he said to them, 'Come with me by yourselves to a quiet place and get some rest.'
> Mark 6:31 NIV

The essence of a retreat is to take some time away from your normal day-to-day life and be with God. It allows you the space to rest, to gain perspective and to regather strength. Think of soldiers retreating from battle before going back out on the field. It also gives us an opportunity to 'detox' from doing and producing, just to be with our own hearts and with God. It's a time to be nourished on a deeper level than some of the more frequent practices give us the opportunity for.

Many of us end up experiencing periods of burnout because our culture is addicted to busyness and productivity. The little drops of retreat we get in regular practices of things like solitude and Sabbath are wonderful, but it's fantastic if we can draw aside most years for an extended time to get away. If you find yourself in one of the more challenging seasons of life listed later in this chapter, apply the relevant suggestions and do the best you can. Something really is better than nothing.

Some ideas for retreats

A retreat can be done anywhere; it doesn't have to involve travelling far or spending lots of money, although of course it can, if that's an option for you. You can go to a dedicated retreat space, look for a quiet cabin or even go camping. You could look into house swapping/sitting as a fantastic and cheap way to get away. I encourage you to creatively explore the options that could be available to you.

If you're brand new to going on retreat, then a guided one can be brilliant. There are many dedicated centres and holidays. Sometimes there are even some that come with a theme such as creativity, silence or poetry. The way they are all set up just lends itself to simplicity and ease. I went to several at a local centre before having the desire or confidence to embark on a solitary retreat. At the in-person retreats I lead, I often have people coming in their fifties and sixties and they have never been on retreat in their whole lives. It's never too late to begin.

You can plan one yourself, maybe with the support of a soul friend or a spiritual director. It doesn't have to be a solitary event. If you do choose to go with others, maybe consider carving out part of it to be spent alone.

Whether you go to a centre or you plan your own, you can choose the length of time that is available to you – it all counts. Whether that's twelve hours, three days or a week, just go with what you've got. I encourage you to discern by considering the season of life you are in and then discussing your options with people in your family, a friend or a spiritual director. A lot of us can feel guilty taking time away or asking for help. On our own, it can be hard to discern what is an appropriate amount of time to go or even money to spend on something like this.

It is ideal to be away from your own home if that's an option, but if it isn't, you can absolutely design a retreat at home. If this is your situation, I advise creating a clear space away from the household and work tasks and doing some simple things to help make the time and space feel set apart and different. You could get a nice new candle, pick some wildflowers or get some lovely food in. There are even lots of digital retreats that are led online; that way you still get the advantage of someone else planning it for you.

Essentially, the point is to carve out some time away from tasks, duties, work and responsibilities just to be with God for some length of extended time. It doesn't have to be complicated or cost a lot of money. Just do what you can to get away with what you have.

Here are some of the ways I have integrated an annual retreat into my life over the years.

I came to faith when I was nineteen and I didn't even hear of going away on retreat until I was a mother of two. I had a day at a local retreat house while my husband had the kids. I would have been about twenty-seven years old, and I think I was away for eight hours. I remember that there was a short time of silence, and I walked around the beautiful gardens and spent time journalling. I recently read back what I had written then and it was significant for me. I felt met by God in that time and received guidance on an issue that we were discerning as a family. I can see now an important seed for the contemplative was sown then.

Is going on a retreat already part of your life? If so, when was the last time you went to one? And do you have the next one booked in? Does going away or staying at home feel more appropriate to you? Do you feel drawn to crafting your own one? Or would you prefer to participate in a guided one? Would you like to go alone, or is there a friend you would like to ask?

I went on to have two more children over the next three years and, apart from a few hours here and there, I didn't get away on a retreat again until we moved to Scotland, and I was in my mid-thirties. Then, it became a regular part of my life. The game changer for me was finding the wonderful episcopal retreat centre The Bield, which I've already mentioned. It was close enough for me to travel to but far enough away that it felt like I was out of my little world. The key takeaway here is that it became realistic, affordable and achievable for me for the season of life I was in. They provided the support and guidance that I needed and offered me enough of something different to help me grow and develop in my faith. It helped me deeply rest and just be with God.

Research places near you; are there ones you could try? Are you drawn to go alone or with others? If alone, can you find a time/place to go? If with others, pray about who to ask and ask them! It's hard enough getting something in the diary for yourself; if you want to go with a friend, it can be even more challenging so look ahead and book in advance.

It was at The Bield that I first encountered spiritual direction and different ways of gathering and praying. It was completely life-changing for me. I learned how to be quiet, how to sit with Scripture and how to discern. I saw and experienced a different way of being in the world and it prepared me for the three days of total silence and solitude that I took last year – one of the most sacred experiences of my life. I'd love to share a bit more about it with you.

My three days of silence and solitude

With the help of my spiritual director I planned and prepared for three days of silence, but I never planned for three days of solitude. I was supposed to be in a retreat centre surrounded by people and supported in my silence, but through various circumstances I ended up alone in a tiny little cabin surrounded by nature. I was undoubtedly led there by God and would not have had the same experience without the simplicity and smallness of my surroundings.

Before this, I had never been truly on my own for even a day. I'm not sure that up until this point I'd ever been silent for more than a few hours. I set strong intentions for my time there. I believe this is very important. As the saying goes: 'Where attention goes, energy flows.' In addition to generally retreating to be with God, I wanted to:

1 Be as open to the Spirit of God in every single way possible. My hope from this intention was to tangibly experience God. My early Christian formation in the Pentecostal tradition gave me a wonderful gift: to expect to experience God. I am so grateful for that. But I noticed that recently I hadn't been living my life in a way that was really open, expectant and receptive to receiving God.
2 Pray to receive healing for my long-standing, chronic pain in my pelvis. The flare-up I was in at that time had been eight weeks of daily pain and movement restriction. I had a sense that as well as being a physical problem, it was also a trauma response.

In my preparation, I predefined my boundaries: I would be totally silent, take no music or phone. Only one book, the Gospel of John, my journal, exercise mat, meditation cushion and simple food. To help embody my intentions, I also prepared by doing a week's physical cleanse beforehand: eating simple, whole foods, taking herbs and getting as much sleep as I could. I believe the physical greatly affects the spiritual. I continued this way of eating on the retreat, and it has actually positively impacted my eating habits ever since. This is an example of how these set-apart times can give us clarity and direction for our everyday lives.

As it was my first time retreating outside of a retreat centre, I set myself a schedule for the three days. At the centre there are set times for prayers and meals, and I always found that helpful. It kept things simple and ordered. This wasn't a set formula, but the timetable that I thought would help me to embody my intentions.

- Wake up – I had no alarm and no control over this. My first realisation when I arrived was that I had made a planning error to not bring one and I didn't like it! If I did it again, I would take an alarm that's not on a phone.
- Journal dump all my thoughts and feelings.
- Gentle movement practice, including helping my body to feel open and receptive.
- Twenty-minute meditation sit (centering prayer).
- Water-ball meditation – imagining the Spirit of God like a ball of water above my head, then going through all of my body, cleansing everything that was spiritually and physically in the way. I ended this by imagining the water going through my hands, which I placed over my pelvis and prayed for healing.
- Breakfast.
- Read one third of John's Gospel and write notes/thoughts.
- Journal dump.
- Invigorating movement practice.
- Twenty-minute meditation (imaginative prayer, going into my heart as a physical landscape and talking to Jesus).
- Water-ball meditation.
- Lunch.
- Go for a walk, read my book or nap.

Faith Habits and How to Form Them

- Journal dump.
- Gentle movement practice.
- Twenty-minute meditation (centering prayer).
- Dinner.
- Walk or read my book.
- 9:30 p.m. – sleep.

> Jesus did many other things as well. If every one of them were written down, I suppose that even the whole world would not have room for the books that would be written.
> John 21:25 NIV

It was only three days, not the thirty-three years that Jesus lived! But so much happened in those three days. When you are alone and silent, time is different somehow. Without any distractions or the normal level of stimulation, the days felt long. I'd like to vulnerably share with you some of the ways that I was changed during that time:

- I experienced the tangible presence of God once while reading the Bible. It was intense, sacred, holy, peaceful and profound. It came out of nowhere and lasted for around two minutes. I wept silent, hot tears and felt it in every cell of my body. This was a massive surprise for me, and it was a significant step to healing my relationship with the Bible. It also ignited the desire and drive to do the Ignatian Spiritual Exercises.
- I loved being on my own, and I loved being silent. I expected to struggle but I didn't. I felt like my true self, and I felt so connected to God and my own heart. At times I felt like a child, doing things I hadn't done for decades like drawing around leaves and marvelling at wildlife.
- I felt massive resistance to every meditation sit. I do not like being still at all! This is also, I believe, the reason I experienced

so much breakthrough. It prompted me to ask a lot of questions about why stillness is so hard for me.
- I experienced times that felt a bit scary, like when I got lost on a walk and I realised no one knew where I was and I had no phone. Also when I went outside to use the toilet at night in the dark. But also the personal fear of facing some uncomfortable truths about myself while in prayer.
- I had three deceased saints come to mind in images while in meditation. They didn't speak to me, but I thanked them in my heart for the inspiration they have been in my life. This moment felt very peaceful and sacred to me as I considered the great cloud of witnesses.
- Lots of memories of good and bad experiences from different times in my life surfaced and I began to deal with things that needed dealing with. I think the way I have been able to be vulnerable in my writing since is a result of that.
- This is the big one: the healing. Over the three days I felt that my pelvis got worse. This was probably a result of all the sitting I did. However, on the last time of prayer, all the elements came together… literally. This sounds like fiction, but it is entirely true. I was doing the water-ball meditation, and it started to rain lightly. The wind blew strongly, and the sun came out. It was hot on my head, and I became intensely aware of the earth beneath me. It was a powerful moment; then I felt the words in my heart: 'It is done.' I couldn't move and I didn't dare believe it. It wasn't instant but as the day continued, my pain became less and less. Before I went to bed that night, it was gone. It had hurt on and off for the last eighteen months and I had been in chronic daily pain for the eight weeks before the retreat. It was and is a miracle. I believe I was healed by God of a physical condition that had traumatic roots. I'll never be able to prove it; I only have my experience.

I was catapulted out of my comfort zone and unexpectedly into one of the best and deepest experiences of my life. I became alive to my own heart, to some of my essence and the childlike qualities of my nature. I became closer to who I have always been. I slowly shed the hats I wear, and it was just me and God.

I hope my story inspires and challenges you. Thank you for bearing witness to it. Our stories are worth telling. Our lives are worth living, wide awake and connected. We all learn things in these times that can't be learned any other way.

In your own retreat practice, I don't think it's advisable to start with something quite this long unless you feel absolutely sure. I built up to the three days with short day-long retreats. I also chose somewhere safe where I could access people and a phone if I needed to. There are places you can go on silent retreat and experience a lot of solitude without having to be totally alone. Are you ready for a more extended retreat? What would you need to do to be able to plan one? Do it!

Pilgrimage

> …a journey made with intentions leave something behind in order to seek God is at the heart of pilgrimage.
> Adele Ahlberg Calhoun[49]

Pilgrimage is a wonderful embodied practice. It's a way of taking an intentional journey with the purpose of encountering God. There has been a real resurgence of interest in pilgrimage over the last few years. Films like *The Way* and BBC documentaries on pilgrimage have brought it to the forefront of people's minds. I knew nothing of pilgrimage until the last few years. People I knew did mission trips but no one I knew did pilgrimages. My image of someone taking a

---

49 A. Ahlberg Calhoun, *Spiritual Disciplines Handbook*, p. 69.

pilgrimage was of a much older person of Catholic faith going to worship at a shrine. It felt entirely irrelevant to me and to my faith at the time.

Even as I've learned more about them, and felt interest and desire spark within me, I've still felt excluded from being able to take part due to finances or time. It is my 'all or nothing' way of thinking that made me exclude myself, rather than anything I was taught directly. I thought things like: 'I can't take six weeks out of life to do the Camino de Santiago, or fly to Israel and do a Holy Land tour, so I guess I'll just have to wait until the kids leave home or I'm retired to experience a pilgrimage.'

To my surprise, I have since discovered that these are not the only options! I began to realise the world – well, the UK where I live, at least – is littered with holy sites. Not only that, but you can set out from your own front door with the heart of a pilgrim. Just like we learn from Adele's definition of pilgrimage above, it's about taking a journey with a heart to encounter God. I'm sure a lot of us can do something with heart posture. What comes to mind for you as you think of pilgrimage? Have you ever done one? What puts you off? What draws you to it?

There are classic pilgrimages such as the ones I referenced earlier. These may be in reach for you and if they are – that's wonderful! Go for it! If you can walk where Jesus walked in the Holy Land or walk the Camino de Santiago or visit holy sites associated with St Francis, Mother Teresa or St Patrick, that's brilliant. Just like the retreats, these can be done alone or with a guide. If something like this isn't realistic for you, then there are still ways you can go on a pilgrimage.

Some accessible ideas for pilgrimage

- Visiting a holy well – they are everywhere! Or any place that has been sacred and part of our rich Christian heritage.
- Catching a bus from your home and then walking to a different church to look around and to pray.

- Visiting a cathedral. Again, you could walk part of the way or travel near or far to get to one.
- A special place in creation, such as a mountain or a waterfall. As well as man-made, holy places all of creation can be viewed as sacred and a place of potential encounter.
- A pilgrimage into your heart via a slow, intentional walk.
- Learning about a saint and seeing their life through the eyes of a pilgrim if you aren't able to leave your home.
- The birthplace, church or workplace of a saint, a ministry or organisation that is special to you.

You could seek specific resources or go on an organised pilgrimage if that is appealing and accessible to you. Or you could design your own to do alone or with a friend.

In 2024, as my fortieth birthday present, I went on a guided pilgrimage in Spain, following the life and story of St Ignatius. I visited the site of his birth and other significant places such as where he had his big accident and had his conversion. We visited holy sites and did walks and bus trips as we went, as well as sharing meals and taking part in daily mass. As someone who is not a Catholic, this was a new and wonderful experience. This was my first 'classic' pilgrimage. It was the first time I had had the money and time to do it.

I had unwittingly attached a lot of hope and expectation to my pilgrimage. I wanted a time of rest and renewal, a time of being held and filled up, and a time of encounter and the rich presence of God. I never even considered that these things wouldn't happen. As an optimist of dangerous levels, my assumption was that I would get what I wanted. It's embarrassing to type this, but I do just exist with this notion that things will go my way and if they don't initially, then I will simply make them. Here are a few unexpected things that happened:

- I woke up on the morning of my flight to discover that I had received some bad news. This set my nervous system on edge and made it difficult for me to leave.
- The weather hit 40°C every single day, with high humidity, and our accommodation had no air conditioning or room fans. This meant I never got more than four or five hours of broken sleep a night and I couldn't get out into the beautiful nature beyond the organised trips of the pilgrimage. This was a barrier to the deep rest and connection to God through nature and solitude that I was expecting.
- The pilgrimage was great in many ways; I met lovely people and loved learning about St Ignatius and visiting key places. But I had expected (there I go again) much more spiritual practice with some moments of group silence and reflections. It was never said that this would be part of it, but I assumed it would be.

Midweek, a friend messaged me to see how it was all going and I had to admit I was struggling. I felt guilty about that. Here I was on this amazing trip and inside I was just disappointed. I had spent all this money, was missing my family and I couldn't even get out and enjoy the place, rest well or feel held spiritually. Nothing I desired was happening.

On the penultimate day, we got to visit the cave where Ignatius spent months 'wrestling his demons'. We held mass in there and I found myself in my own wrestle, practically begging God for a sense of connection. A Mother Teresa quote came to mind while I was in the cave: 'If you want to change the world, go home and love your family.' It felt real and true.

On the final night, mass was held in a small, beautiful room in the Montserrat Basilica. It felt very special; at the closing of the service the quote came back to me very strongly, and with it came a deep sense of God's presence. In that room you can see the back of the Black Madonna, the statue in front of which Ignatius laid down his sword and fully committed to this path. I had a little moment with her too that final night.

Ignatius left a lot of gifts to the Church. The Spiritual Exercises, practices such as the examen, the whole Jesuit order. He also left a principle/practice called Indifference. This is the practice of being able to hold things lightly so we can be truly free to love and serve God and those around us: freedom from disordered attachments to experience a life of true interior freedom. Fr David Fleming puts it this way: 'Everything has the potential of calling forth in us a deeper response to our life in God.'[50]

I wanted rest, connection, nature and spiritual practice. I thought that's what I needed. I got inescapable heat, unmet expectations and the chance to see just how attached I am to things that do not lead me towards freedom.

A week after the trip, I walked and talked with my good friend Ruth and I realised that in the end, it was the perfect Ignatian experience. The very last thing I needed was to get everything I wanted. I needed to see that when things didn't go my way, I could overcome my feelings of disappointment. I still left having met God in the middle of it all, just not how and when I expected. Pilgrimage has a way of surprising and unsettling us. I recommend going with an open heart and mind and letting the journey do its transforming work in you.

In 2018, Jon and I had the incredible opportunity to visit a ministry that had spoken a lot into our hearts. A Place for the Heart is located in North Carolina, and we got there through a combination of prayer, saving every penny that came our way, and the generosity of others... plus the odd miracle! We also needed the support of grandparents who had our children for the best part of a week. I felt an incredible amount of guilt and anxiety at leaving

---

[50] D. Fleming SJ, 'The First Principle and Foundation', The Spiritual Exercises of Ignatius of Loyola: https://www.bc.edu/content/dam/files/offices/ministry/pdf/First%20Principle%20and%20Foundation%20-March%202015%20%282%29.pdf (accessed 20 January 2025).

our children and going so far. I actually made myself ill, but we pressed on with the trip and it was truly transformational. It was also very special to experience it as a couple, as we have had to do most trips individually because of our large, young family. On this trip, I became reacquainted with my own heart after having felt some distance from it. A lot of the things we felt we wanted to offer in ministry were confirmed and we were pushed firmly out of our British comfort zones! I think that when you take a journey, you are able to see things you can't always see in your normal context. It's an opportunity to try things you wouldn't ordinarily be exposed to or brave enough to do and that was certainly my experience. I remember a particularly uncomfortable but powerful experience when we were asked to write a letter to Jesus answering the question he asked Peter: 'Who do you say I am?' That was fine. Then we had to ask God the same question about ourselves, writing down everything we desired God to think of us. Then we had to go around in a circle and say the one that was the hardest for us to believe. I could manage this, too. But the most excruciatingly uncomfortable activity came next. We had to write that thing on a name badge and walk around the room and introduce ourselves to everyone by this identifier. I can still remember my absolute panic at having to do this. I considered changing mine from my very vulnerable statement to one that was easier, but then I figured I spent thousands to go on this pilgrimage, so I might as well go for it. We all just walked around crying our eyes out doing this ultimate icebreaker! Seeing as I managed to do it then, I think I'm brave enough to tell you what I wrote. I still desire it, and still don't feel like it's true, but I believe it more than I did then.

'My name is Emma and I am a good mum.'

While on a pilgrimage, you also end up being in need of something at some point. In our self-sufficient lives, this is very good for us. I mentioned I made myself ill with stress by going on this trip. This manifested itself as an early period, hemorrhaging large amounts of blood and labour-intensity pain. When I arrived, I couldn't stand up straight or act like I was OK. The staff flocked around me with essential oils and heat pads and pain relief. It was very humbling, and I also felt very loved. I spent a day in bed, with little visits from the team, and it was as sacred as the more obvious blessing in other parts of the pilgrimage. A cleverly disguised moment for me to pull into God!

In 2022, my husband and I finally made it to the sacred Scottish island of Iona. We had always wanted to go and had lived in Scotland for five years by that point, but for some reason had never quite managed it. But when some friends came over from the United States to see it, we felt challenged and inspired to do the same – especially as it was far closer for us! The encouragement and example from friends empowered us to make it happen. We had to take all our own food and sleep in the cheapest pod we could find, and it was wonderful. A missionary friend ended up gifting us with £100 so we could have a beautiful special meal when we were there. She knows all too well what it's like to do everything on a budget. The kindness of friends makes such a big difference.

We experienced, deeply and tangibly, what the Celts referred to as a 'thin place'. This is a place where the veil between heaven and earth feels thinner. It's a mystical and almost indescribable experience, but I will give it a go.

We had been inspired by the Iona community that live on the island and the saints who used to live there, but nothing could have prepared us for getting off that boat. As soon as we stepped our feet onto Iona we were flooded with emotions, like the feeling you have when you look into the eyes of a newborn or see an epic sunset. I can remember a spiritual clarity overtaking my being. Everything came into focus; it was like we couldn't take it in enough. We just kept saying WOW.

We had preordered a fish a few days earlier from a local fisherman, for the mighty price of £5. I still don't know what type of fish it was because we couldn't specify – it was just what they had caught that day. The box with the fish was waiting for us when we got off the boat. It sat there with our name on it, and we hadn't even paid for it yet. We spent the whole time in a haze of delight, wandering about and trying to soak it all in. We went to the high point, to the church, to the bay. I may have even risked a bit of a skinny dip. I had to stay in the water a bit longer than I wanted while I waited for some kayakers to move past. They literally came out of nowhere! It was very special. Another truly bonding experience in our marriage.

Once a year feels like a generous and realistic frequency to plan a pilgrimage and I hope from the suggestions above you can see how scalable it is. You could take a thirty-minute walk to a holy well and spend an hour in contemplation, or you could do a month touring the Holy Land. I encourage you to use your imagination and find a way to take part. And if you don't want to, just like all the other practices, let it go.

Mission/service of others

…Love your neighbour as yourself.
Mark 12:31 NIV

This subject is so vast, and often our mission and service are worked out within the context of our daily lives. Most people I know care for and serve others constantly and have full plates. If that's you, please don't let the thought of mission be like another weight to carry. Instead, this is a chance to pause and do something each year with real intention – something set apart. It's a great opportunity to join with others to serve, maybe doing something as a family or with friends, or with a small group or even church.

While there is some crossover, mission differs from a pilgrimage, which has the specific intention of taking a journey to seek after and encounter God. This is about serving others in a tangible way.

I encourage you to seek out the heart of this within your current capacity. It could be a dedicated time of prayer, financial giving, making something slowly and lovingly for someone in need. If you yourself are in a deep place of need and just can't, then don't! It's OK. You may be in a place where you need to rest, heal and receive. Equally, if you are sick or in great need but you want to incorporate mission, and you feel it won't make your situation worse, then go for it! There is never a formula and never a right or wrong answer. There is only a journey of walking with God and doing the best you can at the time.

As I have been writing this book, I have realised this is the area most lacking in my yearly practices, so I am planning to do something specific next year. This is another reason it's wonderful to have a rule of life and a sense of intentionality when walking out our faith. It can help us look at our lives with honesty and see any changes we want to make.

Ideas for mission/service

Going to another country to help those in need seems an obvious place to start, particularly as it's what we most strongly associate with 'mission'. I would implore you to please try to avoid organisations that are involved in mission that looks more like colonialism. As Christians we do not have a good history with some of the mission work that has come from the West. If I am giving time or money, and am therefore in a position of power, I'm mindful to not fall into the easy trap of a 'saviour complex'. This can do more harm than good to both you and the people you set out to support. If you engage in this kind of service, it's also good to make sure you have somewhere in your life where you are the lower hand and are the one in need. If you notice, Jesus did both. He served others and he humbled himself to need others. The latter can be much harder – it's a real ego crusher!

Helping at a local food bank, through volunteering or donations.

Volunteering at a soup kitchen or free meal organisation is a good way to serve. You don't have to be front-facing if this feels difficult for you. If you have a leadership role normally, it's a good idea to humble yourself and just get in the background, washing the pots or supporting the other volunteers.

Service at another church. Is there a church local to you that has an ageing population? Could a few of you see if they need a hand with some practical or physical jobs?

You could also approach your local council and see if they need help with litter-picking, painting or weeding. Ask yourself the question: Where is there a need that God might be asking me to meet? Hand to the plough, good Samaritan-type stuff... Jesus was pretty into it. What is some sort of mission you could do this year? Is there something really specific that you feel drawn to create? Or is there something already happening that you can join? What draws you to mission? What puts you off?

Practices for different stages of life

For everything there is a season, and a time for every matter under heaven.
Ecclesiastes 3:1 NRSV

Some disciples came to see Abba Poemen and said to him: 'Tell us, when we see brothers dozing during the sacred office, should we pinch them so they will stay awake?' And the old man said to them: 'Actually, if I saw a brother sleeping, I would put his head on my knees and let him rest.'
Joan Chittister, *Illuminated Life*[51]

Ever been through a really tough time? Ever had a circumstance or illness happen and every practice just goes totally out of the window along with most of your sanity? I know I have several times over the years. There are certain seasons of life that are so significant or different that they deserve special mention and a lot of the 'normal rules/advice' just don't cut it. This isn't an exhaustive list but here are some I would love to take the time to cover:

- Practices for parents of young children
- Substantial caring duties of another person/people
- Chronic illness/pain
- Season of transition: geographic/divorce/perimenopause

---

[51] J. Chittister, *Illuminated Life: Monastic Wisdom for Seekers of Light* (Maryknoll, NY: Orbis Books, 2000), p. 113.

- Intense study/workload
- You're just not coping well and you don't know why

If you don't find yourself in any of these seasons of life just now, I encourage you to read through them anyway. There will be people in your family, church or wider community experiencing these trials, and reading about them will help you to have increased compassion and love them well.

If you are in any of the seasons I have listed, then I just want to say, I see you. God sees you. You are completely loved and enough just as you are. I invite you to take a deep, slow, full, breath in and a big loud sigh as you exhale. You can take all that pressure off immediately! I've observed through my own life and the lives of other people that when we face a challenging season, there are three common and pretty unhelpful responses. They will largely depend on the kind of person you are and how you process things; feel free to add your own:

1. Just carrying on regardless! Ignoring all your obvious limitations, you may push yourself into major stress and make unrealistic demands of your body. It's the classic 'keep calm and carry on'! Then, just to make it a bit more unhelpful, that attitude can become 'spiritualised'. The Bible says 'rejoice always' so some people will bypass their real feelings and refuse any help. Been here, and I was such a delight to be around…
2. Giving up on your hopes and desires for yourself. You may think and be feeling things like 'what's the point?', 'there's no time', 'everything always goes wrong', 'when I dare to make any plans they get thwarted' and 'I can't handle the disappointment'. To top it off, you're left feeling a bit resentful. This is my most common response; I really struggle with any feeling of limitation or not being able to do what I want.

3 Becoming a total martyr. You may start to find your identity and even pride in your struggle. You could even use the circumstances as a way to hide. Thoughts could be things like 'I don't get to do these sorts of things now because of such and such, but I don't mind' – but everyone can tell, you do mind. I actually don't tend to do this, but I've seen it enough.

Although all of these coping mechanisms are completely understandable, none of them ultimately serve us, make us more Christlike or help us to grow. I would like to offer an alternative response to any challenging season of life. It is really simple, but also takes real humility and intentionality to put in place. It is simply to let go of unrealistic expectations and stay close to God through realistic and flexible practices. That means being kind to yourself and seeking help where you can. It means taking the time, maybe with a soul friend or spiritual director, to figure out what, from your responsibilities, you can let go of and prioritise what is most helpful to you.

Let's go through the categories individually to try to flesh out that alternative response and look at some micro ways you can keep your identity and your sanity in these times.

For parents of young children

As a woman who gave birth to four children in just over six years, I have a very special place in my heart for this group of people. In fact, somewhere in my disorganised filing cabinet I have 70,000 words – an entire book I wrote over the ten years that my kids were young – all about the spiritual challenges of early parenting. Maybe one day I will rework it, and it will see the light of day!

A joyous and wonderful season? YES. But also challenging, right? We can absolutely love raising young children and still find it hard. The lack of sleep, constant noise and interruption, caring, feeding, being vigilant, the unreasonable tantrums and demands – all of this can take its toll. Even if you take to parenting like the proverbial duck to water, it's still a significant lifestyle change. All of this makes it a tough season to flourish in contemplative practice!

I was in this season of life for a very long time. One child started sleeping through the night and then we had another baby. One child got potty-trained and weaned off a dummy, just in time for us to go through it again with the next child. I tried so many things to keep me connected to God in this season. I strived and gave up, I explored and I researched. I tried and I failed, and I tried again, mainly because I just couldn't accept that things were different now. Once I finally did, it ended up being simpler than I thought. It came down to a mindset shift. There isn't anything we need to 'do' to be more spiritual or more connected to God apart from awaken to the fact that we are already inseparable. God is so very close; in every fibre of our being, in fact. Eventually I learned to incorporate tiny, adaptable practices and to grow in becoming flexible and adaptable. Here are my top suggestions for parents of young children:

- If you are a single parent, I encourage you, where it's possible, to get some support around you. If you are part of a couple, please try to share the load, mental and physical. Whatever your gender, try to not leave it to one person to carry an unrealistic share of the tasks; that just isn't fair. If you aren't pulling your weight then start, and if you are pulling too much weight (ahem, the martyrs!), stop it and ask for help! I was so blessed with this; Jon and I have always shared the load. This is something that is going to be individual and depend on employed workload, general capacity and natural personality, as well as the kind of home culture you grew up in and your inbuilt perception of gender roles. But whatever your circumstances, have a good look at them, and consciously

decide and work towards something that feels healthy and sustainable in your specific setup.
- Acceptance always goes a long way, but it's absolutely fundamental here. Life won't be the same for a while; if you need to grieve that, then do so and don't feel bad about it. Change even in the midst of great joy can bring a sense of loss, or a missing of what was before. This is totally fine and doesn't mean you don't absolutely love your children.
- God is EVERYWHERE. If you didn't always recognise this, now is the time – PRAY! Ask God to reveal Godself to you all the time. In nature, in your baby's smile, as you eat your food or light a candle or chat with a friend. This is where contemplative prayer really comes into its own; anywhere you are paying attention with love can become prayer.
- Ask yourself if you still want to have 'a rule' for this season of life. A lot of people, especially women, can lose their identity in parenthood. We aren't equipped well or valued very well in our society for the work of parenting. I personally didn't know how to navigate the many changes, and I felt bad for struggling so I ended up feeling a bit stuck.
- Even though it's going to look wildly different, I wouldn't give up on pursuing some kind of intentional spirituality. If you need convincing, then just ponder this: when you are more aware of your connection to God and receiving that love and delight, you will be more yourself and more able to show that love to those around you.

Here are some examples of daily practices. But remember, if these don't sit well with you, let them be a launchpad to think of your own.

- Morning – Wake with your baby. Have breath prayer cards by your bed; pick one up and repeat the prayer a few times. There

are some examples of breath prayers back in the daily practices section.
- Another idea is just to pause as you hear that alarm (or baby) go off, and take a micro pause, remembering Gods presence within you and around you, whatever is going on. This would just be five or ten seconds.
- Lunchtime – Set an alarm and read the Lord's Prayer or something from a daily prayer book. This takes the pressure off you, as you don't have to come up with the words. Let the prayers of others carry and uphold you.
- Before bed – Do a really quick examen, either just in your head or in a journal. One thing that was hard, one thing you are grateful for. This can be done in literally two minutes if that's all you have the time or energy for.
- Try to schedule in the seasonal review; children change so quickly that there might be practices that were out of the question in spring, but now that it's autumn, you can reintroduce them. If you need a bit of headspace for this, then enlist some help or do it during your child's nap time.
- Try to find an occasional bit of solitude, time with a friend or time for fun in whatever way you can. You need it; you are still a person with your own needs and that is more than OK. Again, view this in your context; maybe it can be planned in, maybe you need to grab it when you can. However you do it is fine – it's all valid.

They say that comparison is the thief of joy, and they are right! I implore you to work towards letting go of comparison. So what if Shirley from marketing can work full time, be on the international ministry team and have three young kids? Or if Sandra has chosen to quit work and spends all day crocheting and homeschooling? You are who you are, with your capacity and personality and situation. Comparison isn't helpful for anyone, but in this season of life, you just can't afford to waste time on it AT ALL.

When the best-laid plans all go to pot, feel your feelings. Sad? Disappointed? Angry? Ashamed? Hopeless? Indifferent? All valid. Read *Domestic Monastery* by Ronald Rolheiser;[52] it's another one of those small books crammed full of wisdom. He has so much incredible stuff to say on this topic. Among other highly valuable insights, he talks about how your baby's cry or toddler's demands can become your monastery bell. Just keep showing up to your daily life, and know that God is with you in and through it all.

For those with caring duties

Apart from the context of young kids, I have no personal experience of this, just a lot of observation. Maybe you have an elderly parent living with you, maybe your partner has mental health challenges, maybe you have a child with additional needs. Situations like these can be more like a lifestyle than a season, but the response remains much the same.

Try to let go of unrealistic expectations and stay close to God through realistic and flexible practices. Choose things that work with the time you have available. If it is very limited, then look for things that can be incorporated into your caring responsibilities. That could be prayers you place around the house or the soaking in of beauty around you on walks. It's more about the heart than anything else.

Be kind to yourself and seek help if and where you can. Having such heavy caring responsibilities is really tough, and even though it is a gift and a reflection of the selfless nature of Christ, it can feel relentless. I have a friend whose partner has severe depression and although she loves him deeply, it is tough to be around that struggle

---

52 R. Rolheiser, *Domestic Monastery* (London: Darton, Longman & Todd Ltd, 2019).

all the time. She needs to get out and have fun when she can to keep her own mental health stable. It isn't disloyal to the person you are caring for to be impacted by them. Take some time to ask yourself: What is it you find hard? What practice might help you find some restoration?

Figure out what you can let go of and prioritise what is most helpful to you. Somebody, or multiple people, may need a lot of your time and you probably have other domestic and professional responsibilities, too. Is there anything, anything at all that you can offload or let go of? What is the most important to you? What is your favourite way to feel connected to and nourished by God? Is it in nature, praying with others, in solitude, in Scripture, in church, in creativity? What is one small way you could prioritise that in your day or week? Use your imagination to pray and seek support.

Remember, just like the parent of young children, you are a person too. Caring for yourself is necessary and right and good. It will ultimately be better for the person you are caring for, too. So again, I invite you to shelve the guilt.

For those with chronic illness

This is a big topic; I can barely scratch the surface in such a short section. And as I'm sure you've already discerned, I am not a doctor or a mental health professional. But I do work in the wellness industry, and I have friends who do live within these categories, so I know enough to know this: if you aren't well, you do not have the same capacity as someone who is. As I am typing this part of the book, I have a pelvis injury (I initially wrote this section before I went on my transformational three-day retreat). I am not working at the pace I normally do, the pain is distracting and I am having to take more breaks to keep getting up and move around. I feel grumpy and frustrated, and this is just a temporary injury. Some of you are battling ME or cancer or depression. Whatever you're facing, it has an effect – plain and simple. This doesn't mean your life has any less value or can't be equally as wonderful; it just isn't the same. I humbly offer here my simple thoughts on this.

Try to let go of unrealistic expectations and stay close to God through realistic and flexible practices. You may not be able to plan ahead, but see how you are each day and work within your capacity: try breath prayer, nature, beauty, prayer for others, imaginative prayer, creativity, things that remind you of your inherent worthiness outside of anything you can produce or the 'wellness' within your mind or body.

Be kind to yourself and seek help if and where you can. If you are in this category and you are reading this book, thank you so much for investing your precious trust and energy in my words. I pray that they serve you in some way. If you are reading these words and this has never affected you, please remember and serve people with kindness who are dealing with these often hidden, debilitating and on-the-rise issues. Remember, love is our greatest call as followers of Christ.

Figure out what you can let go of and prioritise what is most helpful to you. I will just say that if it is mental health issues that you are struggling with, you may want support from a trained professional. It can be so difficult to have the motivation or the clarity when you are dealing with poor mental health.

Your worth is inherent. Your reflection of God is unmarred by your illness. The love and care and delight of God over you is complete. Never forget it. Fight to remember it. Write it over your heart and on your doorposts. We all need you; you teach us so much. I'm sorry for all the ways you are discredited, overlooked and forgotten, both by society in general and by the Church. If at all possible, consider walking away from any toxic relationships or churches that diminish your worth or create extra stress for you.

Contemplate the suffering Christ. I was formed to always be focusing on the risen Christ, the victorious Christ. These are images of Christ to behold too, of course. But Christ also suffered – physically, emotionally and spiritually. You can seek comfort and remember his companionship and understanding in your suffering. He is close to the broken-hearted.

For those in a time of transition

A season of transition can be any number of things: geographic, divorce, perimenopause, evolving faith. Life in a monastery with a rule of life that is fixed is protected from some of these transitions. For better or worse, the routine and the practices are fixed. You're single and you live in one place. For the rest of us, transition is going to happen at some time. Another word for transition is change. In fact, every time there's a change in season or we age, we get a mini practice at this, by having to adapt to that change. It can be very upsetting and unsettling, depending on the type of transition. But all types of change call for the same thing: that some of our practices will have to flex, and some of them we can hopefully keep the same to help anchor us in this time. Below are my thoughts on what can help us keep our sense of 'groundedness' in a season of transition.

Let go of unrealistic expectations and stay close to God through realistic and flexible practices. I am in the beginning of perimenopause, and the symptoms are endless and inconsistent. I no longer have the same capacity as I did, and we have had to make some practical changes in our home to reflect this. For example, I have to be stricter with my bedtime or I find I just don't cope well. Jon now contributes more to holding everyone's schedule, sometimes called the 'mental load' of a household. This was a role I did with ease and happiness before, but now that I'm experiencing a reduced capacity, I've had to ask for help. When we moved from Cornwall to Scotland, I experienced a total change of environment and a change of faith; I developed totally new practices to help with this. I have maintained some long-distance friendships, but I also had to put myself out there and spend energy on creating new ones. I had to stay close to God through beauty and nature and journalling while I was wrestling with doctrine and belief. As you transition, what do you need to let go of that can't remain the same? What practices can you keep to anchor you?

Be kind to yourself and seek help if and where you can. Change affects us all differently. How are you experiencing it? Is there a friend or family member who can support you? Take time to sit and reflect honestly, either alone or with a friend. Is there any way that you are being unkind to yourself in this season? What could you do to restore that kindness and self-compassion? Remember Jesus mourned and withdrew and responded differently to different seasons of his life. We aren't meant to be robots unaffected by our lives. Actually, when we ignore our feelings and emotions, they can be stored in our bodies. We have to face them and feel them so we can release them and move on. There has unfortunately been some terrible teaching on this in the Church, where Scripture has been taken out of context – such as 'rejoice always' being taken literally! Some people don't feel they can grieve or be sad... it's well meant I'm sure, but entirely unhelpful.

Figure out your priorities and the things that are no longer helpful. Are there any ways you can support your physical health as you transition, and are exposed to more stress? Could you get a bit more sleep, talk to someone about how you're feeling or eat more nourishing foods? Simple, practical things can sometimes be the most spiritual. Remember, when times are hard, our whole being is affected.

Finally, remember that seasons of transition do end, so your circumstances are likely to only be temporary.

For periods of intense study or heavy workload

With a big book deadline looming, I feel right in the middle of this intense workload season. I also still have the constraints of my normal, crazy, glorious life. When you are studying or working a lot, you might find that you have very little space or capacity in your spiritual life for any kind of study. It might be good to find ways to connect with God that don't require any heavy reading or concentrating. Finding God in nature is a wonderful antidote to a lot of work/study.

Again, it's a good time to let go of unrealistic expectations and stay close to God through realistic and flexible practices. If your schedule is changeable, adapt your practices accordingly. It's important to be kind to yourself and to seek help if and where you can.

Consider looking to non-classical practices to bring balance to the extra workload. If your mind is being pushed and overloaded with work, think about what calms the mind and moves you away from stress. These are the things that have a restorative effect, such as a slow prayerful walk, or some *visio divina* – which is a way of looking at an image and contemplating it, allowing God to speak to you through it. Traditionally this is done with religious icons, but it can be with any picture or out in nature.

If it's an intense period and it involves lots of other people, maybe increase the solitude. If it's a lonely busy period, maybe move towards group activities. Try to bring in a bit of balance. Remember, this season will end too!

For those who aren't coping and don't know why

In some ways I think this can be one of the most difficult seasons to deal with or to know how to handle. Nothing is actually 'wrong' per se, but you're just not doing well. Maybe it's apathy and lack of motivation. Maybe you feel sad or really overwhelmed by little things that wouldn't normally bother you. Maybe you're feeling some dissatisfaction or disappointment with the way things are going in your life. Maybe you feel sensitive and triggered by every small thing. Maybe you're just a bit 'blah'!

The first thing to say is, who doesn't feel like this at some point? I'm not sure people spell it out enough. Sometimes we can experience life as just being a bit boring or rubbish. Sometimes God feels distant, there's a lot of going through the motions and it all gets a bit much.

Letting go of unrealistic expectations and staying close to God through realistic and flexible practices will help in this time. You may notice this has been number one in every category – that's because it's always relevant, simple, yet difficult to do. If you are feeling rubbish, you are likely to have a reduced capacity. You may find that the ways you normally find life-giving just aren't working and you need to try some new practices.

Make sure you're being kind to yourself and seek help if and where you can. Figure out what you can let go of and prioritise what is most helpful to you. The regular practice of the examen will really help with this. What is feeding your soul, bringing you life and hope? Can you incorporate more of that? What is depleting you, and draining the life out of you? Can you reduce that? A soul friend or a spiritual director will be able to help you discern these things. You can see here how the practices begin to work together.

I want to close this section with a special mention and reminder to those who find themselves in a larger season of life that is really difficult. First, try to do something to reflect the natural season, because in difficult times it's so important to care for ourselves, especially if there doesn't seem to be the time. Second, I really encourage you to be excessively kind to yourself. Cheer yourself on, or comfort yourself like you would a really good friend who is having a hard time.

Whatever season of life you find yourself in, I hope something in the simple ideas offered above ignite a spark of hope in you.

Practices for your current spiritual state

Here I'm addressing two opposite and extreme spiritual states: flourishing and the dark night. In reality, we mainly sit somewhere between the two. Although one of these seasons is clearly more appealing than the other one, they both have things to teach us if we make the effort to engage with them.

Flourishing

On the surface, everything is going well in your life and things are looking up. In many ways, that is reflected under the surface, too. That is great – my goodness, we don't want things to be difficult all the time! However, I have noticed a pattern over the years – I can become apathetic spiritually when everything is going well in my natural circumstance and all my needs are met. I have to work harder to 'need God' when on the surface I don't. This is possibly one of the things that Jesus is referring to when he says it is easier for a camel to pass through the eye of a needle than for a rich man to enter heaven. It is simply harder to need God and live in a posture of humility when we are really successful or have all our needs met. We see this in the Church and wider culture with the fall of so many incredibly successful leaders. It can be hard to resist pride.

Conversely, when I am in a tough season, I tend to pray and seek God more. It's annoying that it's like this, but I've observed it in the lives of those around me, too. The Church at large tends to flourish on the margins and under persecution – far more than it does when it's the religion of power and prominence. This is why we have the wisdom of the desert mothers and fathers, because they saw how once the Church had power, it began to become corrupt and lose its way. It led them to flee towards self-imposed hardship for the sake of their spirituality. I'm not saying this is something we have to actually do, but it is good to understand the desire.

A flourishing spiritual life doesn't always go hand in hand with a flourishing natural life. Be careful to not confuse the two. When I was experiencing the two years of intermittent chronic pain in my back and pelvis, I was driven to despair at times. But my goodness, it broke down my attachments to security, survival, power and control in a way perfect health could never have done. It exposed my broken coping mechanisms that actually create distance between me and God, between me and my truest self.

Dark night of the soul

A period of spiritual desolation suffered by a mystic in which all sense of consolation is removed.
Oxford English Dictionary[53]

I don't know how to scale or rate this. How can you? What officially classifies as a 'dark night'? Is it the length? Is it the intensity? Do we need to despair to the point of death? What constitutes a mystic? All I know is that a lot of the ancient and modern-day saints have documented experiencing 'dark nights of the soul'. St John of the Cross, Mother Teresa, Julian of Norwich, St Francis, St Ignatius – they all seem to have had different experiences. St John of the Cross was wrongly imprisoned and tortured and had times of utter spiritual desolation in his cell, as well as glorious times of union with God. Julian of Norwich documents having years in her cell

---

53 'dark night of the soul', *Oxford English Dictionary*: https://www.oed.com/search/dictionary/?scope=Entries&q=dark%20night%20of%20the%20soul&tl=true (accessed 20 January 2025).

when she felt entirely desolate and unable to pray or access the presence of God. Mother Teresa's journals reveal that she couldn't sense the presence of God for many years. You can see the dark night theme here, yet no two experiences are the same! Even so, all these people lived extraordinary, God-soaked lives that still speak to and inspire us today. Jesus himself felt the desolation of not being able to connect to God's presence on the cross.

This can be part of the spiritual journey for some people. If nothing else, it's helpful to know that it's normal and if you do find yourself in one of these dark nights, you're in good company. My sense is that this isn't something we should ever be seeking, but we probably can't avoid it. Allow yourself to be in it, seeking support and trusting that even if you have no idea where God is, remember God is right there. You will get through it!

Personally, my only minor experience of this was the years I was wrestling with my theological beliefs. I often felt very lost and alone and I really didn't know where God was in it all. With hindsight, I can see God was always right there and without that season, I almost certainly wouldn't be where I am now. From a rule of life perspective, you could treat this much like any other different season, with kindness and grace. Lean into the spiritual companions around you and some life-giving practices and rhythms to keep you grounded. Reading the accounts of others who have been through this or contemplating the suffering of Christ could also be helpful practices. This too shall pass.

Part 3
THE WORKBOOK

How to pull it all together

As you start to walk on the way, the way appears.
Rumi[54]

Well done – you've done it! We've journeyed together across a whole year, and hopefully you have picked up bits and pieces along the way that you can use. Now it's time to look back over everything you've learned, planned and reflected on and put it together into your very own set of faith habits – your very own 'rule of life'.

We have been on such an amazing journey together. We've delved right back into the ancient times of the desert mothers and fathers. We've explored some of the monks, saints and mystics from different eras. And most importantly, you've reviewed your own life and learned about a massive array of rhythms and practices and how you can apply them. It's now time for the fun bit – to put it all together and craft your rule of life: this living, breathing document that will pull together all the pieces and give you that framework, that trellis for your life to flourish on.

The title of my online community is The Prayer Orchard. This brings to mind beauty and fruit and trees and open space. I would love my rule of life to reflect that, but I'm a straightforward chart and table kinda girl. I'm going to just list in a very logical, boring table a few examples of rules of life from different friends so you can see how it could look.

---

[54] C. Barks and J. ad-Din Muhammad ar-Rumi, *A Year with Rumi: Daily Readings* (Harper San Francisco, 2006), p. 130.

Case study: four people's rules of life

Emma, online contemplative community leader and movement teacher

	Spring	Summer	Autumn	Winter
Daily	Examen Centering prayer Morning journalling Gratitude journal Sea swimming	Examen Centering prayer Morning journalling Gratitude journal Sea swimming	Examen Centering prayer – not quite every day Ignatian Spiritual Exercises Gratitude journal	Examen Centering prayer – not quite every day Ignatian Spiritual Exercises Gratitude journal
Weekly	Weekly journalling Examen in community Sabbath Church Time in nature	Weekly journalling Examen in community Sabbath Church Time in nature	Weekly journalling Examen in community Sabbath Church Time in nature Spiritual direction with Amy	Weekly journalling Examen in community Sabbath Church Time in nature Spiritual direction with Amy
Monthly	Seeing Phileena for spiritual direction Half day of solitude Time with a soul friend Family adventure day in nature	Seeing Phileena for spiritual direction Half day of solitude Time with a soul friend Family adventure day in nature	Day of silence and solitude Time with a soul friend	Day of silence and solitude Time with a soul friend
Seasonal	A 7-day cleanse Review and tweak rule of life Deep clean of house	Review and tweak rule of life No cleanse Solitary climb on mountain	Family adventure day in nature A 10-day cleanse Review and tweak rule of life Deep clean of house and sort clothes Seeing Phileena for spiritual direction	Family adventure day in nature A 7-day cleanse Review and tweak rule of life Seeing Phileena for spiritual direction
Yearly	Supported International Justice Mission	Went to a Christian festival	3-day silence and solitude retreat	Away in cabin to write this book!

Jon, 24-7 Prayer community leader and charity worker

	Spring	Summer	Autumn	Winter
Daily	Silence, stillness & solitude each morning. I consider this a 'container practice' to hold space for centering prayer, Bible reading, devotional reading, journalling with God, early morning walk in nature. There are slight differences each morning but will contain one or some of these.	Silence, stillness & solitude each morning. I consider this a 'container practice' to hold space for centering prayer, Bible reading, devotional reading, journalling with God, early morning walk in nature. There are slight differences each morning but will contain one or some of these.	Silence, stillness & solitude each morning. I consider this a 'container practice' to hold space for centering prayer, Bible reading, devotional reading, journalling with God, early morning walk in nature. There are slight differences each morning but will contain one or some of these.	Silence, stillness & solitude each morning. I consider this a 'container practice' to hold space for centering prayer, Bible reading, devotional reading, journalling with God, early morning walk in nature. There are slight differences each morning but will contain one or some of these.
	Midday prayer. Alarm on phone is set. Lord's Prayer (NZ Book of Common Prayer version) or my own simple prayer to realign.	Midday prayer. Alarm on phone is set. Lord's Prayer (NZ Book of Common Prayer version) or my own simple prayer to realign.	Midday prayer. Alarm on phone is set. Lord's Prayer (NZ Book of Common Prayer version) or my own simple prayer to realign.	Midday prayer. Alarm on phone is set. Lord's Prayer (NZ Book of Common Prayer version) or my own simple prayer to realign.
	Family meal around the table.	Family meal around the table.	Family meal around the table.	Family meal around the table.
Weekly	Physical activity of some kind. Aim for 3 times a week – a longer walk, run, bike, surf or paddle.	Physical activity of some kind. Aim for 3 times a week – a longer walk, run, bike, surf or paddle.	Physical activity of some kind. Aim for 3 times a week – a longer walk, run, bike, surf or paddle.	Physical activity of some kind. Aim for 3 times a week – a longer walk, run, bike, surf or paddle.
	Creative activity of some kind at least 3 times a week – play guitar, write, photography.	Creative activity of some kind at least 3 times a week – play guitar, write, photography.	Creative activity of some kind at least 3 times a week – play guitar, write, photography.	Creative activity of some kind at least 3 times a week – play guitar, write, photography.
	Join an Order of the Mustard Seed prayer watch	Join an Order of the Mustard Seed prayer watch	Join an Order of the Mustard Seed prayer watch	Join an Order of the Mustard Seed prayer watch
	Sunday gathering with church community	Sunday gathering with church community	Sunday gathering with church community	Sunday gathering with church community
	Midweek gathering with church community	Midweek gathering with church community	Midweek gathering with church community	Midweek gathering with church community
	Early morning prayer twice a week with church community	Early morning prayer twice a week with church community	Early morning prayer twice a week with church community	Early morning prayer twice a week with church community
	Sunday examen with Prayer Orchard	Sunday examen with Prayer Orchard	Sunday examen with Prayer Orchard	Sunday examen with Prayer Orchard
	Sabbath	Sabbath	Sabbath	Sabbath

Faith Habits and How to Form Them

	Spring	Summer	Autumn	Winter
Monthly	Receive spiritual direction Family day out/adventure Solo day out, usually to a soulful place such as the coast, forests or mountains, to pray, write, surf, hike, nourish my soul. Follow monthly rhythm with church community – this includes gathering around the table to share food and walking/immersing in nature.	Receive spiritual direction Family day out/adventure Solo day out, usually to a soulful place such as the coast, forests or mountains, to pray, write, surf, hike, nourish my soul. Follow monthly rhythm with church community – this includes gathering around the table to share food and walking/immersing in nature.	Receive spiritual direction Family day out/adventure Solo day out, usually to a soulful place such as the coast, forests or mountains, to pray, write, surf, hike, nourish my soul. Follow monthly rhythm with church community – this includes gathering around the table to share food and walking/immersing in nature.	Receive spiritual direction Family day out/adventure Solo day out, usually to a soulful place such as the coast, forests or mountains, to pray, write, surf, hike, nourish my soul. Follow monthly rhythm with church community – this includes gathering around the table to share food and walking/immersing in nature.
Seasonal	Observe Lent. Different practices each year but include a specific Lent book for reflection. Embrace each season and its nuances and characteristics. Acknowledge the change and transition, observe changes in energy and pace.	Embrace each season and its nuances and characteristics. Acknowledge the change and transition, observe changes in energy and pace.	Embrace each season and its nuances and characteristics. Acknowledge the change and transition, observe changes in energy and pace.	Observe Advent. Different practices each year but will include a specific Advent book for reflection. Consecrate the new year in prayer with community and time in solitude. Embrace each season and its nuances and characteristics. Acknowledge the change and transition, observe changes in energy and pace.
Yearly	Attend a conference, festival and/or retreat (or a few if possible). This is different each year. I will seek and discern where the invitations from God are leading me.	Attend a conference, festival and/or retreat (or a few if possible). This is different each year. I will seek and discern where the invitations from God are leading me.	Attend a conference, festival and/or retreat (or a few if possible). This is different each year. I will seek and discern where the invitations from God are leading me.	Retake Order of the Mustard seed vows Attend a conference, festival and/or retreat (or a few if possible). This is different each year. I will seek and discern where the invitations from God are leading me.

Faith Habits and How to Form Them

Vicky, poet, artist, spiritual director and charity worker

	Spring	Summer	Autumn	Winter
Daily	Ignatian Spiritual Exercises, praying the psalms, breath prayers	Ignatian Spiritual Exercises, praying the psalms, breath prayers	Ignatian Spiritual Exercises, praying the psalms, breath prayers	Ignatian Spiritual Exercises, praying the psalms, breath prayers
	Writing/journalling, ongoing poetry & illustration projects	Writing/journalling, ongoing poetry & illustration projects	Writing/journalling, ongoing poetry & illustration projects	Writing/journalling, ongoing poetry & illustration projects
	Work with children's charity & other organisations who work for justice	Work with children's charity & other organisations who work for justice	Work with children's charity & other organisations who work for justice	Work with children's charity & other organisations who work for justice
	Reading/research for personal interest and leading courses... and just for joy	Reading/research for personal interest and leading courses... and just for joy	Reading/research for personal interest and leading courses... and just for joy	Reading/research for personal interest and leading courses... and just for joy
	Daily walks in nature, savouring the seasons, seeking everyday wonders	Daily walks in nature, savouring the seasons, seeking everyday wonders	Daily walks in nature, savouring the seasons, seeking everyday wonders	Daily walks in nature, savouring the seasons, seeking everyday wonders
Weekly	Writing, sketching, playing ukulele (badly and joyfully!)	Writing, sketching, playing ukulele (badly and joyfully!)	Writing, sketching, playing ukulele (badly and joyfully!)	Writing, sketching, playing ukulele (badly and joyfully!)
	Participating in weekly prayer rhythm in church community, participating in spiritual accompaniment for the Spiritual Exercises	Participating in weekly prayer rhythm in church community, participating in spiritual accompaniment for the Spiritual Exercises	Participating in weekly prayer rhythm in church community, participating in spiritual accompaniment for the Spiritual Exercises	Participating in weekly prayer rhythm in church community, participating in spiritual accompaniment for the Spiritual Exercises
	Involvement with local food bank & other volunteering organisations	Involvement with local food bank & other volunteering organisations	Involvement with local food bank & other volunteering organisations	Involvement with local food bank & other volunteering organisations
	Offering spiritual accompaniment/ hospitality of the heart to others (formal and informal)	Offering spiritual accompaniment/ hospitality of the heart to others (formal and informal)	Offering spiritual accompaniment/ hospitality of the heart to others (formal and informal)	Offering spiritual accompaniment/ hospitality of the heart to others (formal and informal)
	Course preparation, small group involvement	Course preparation, small group involvement	Course preparation, small group involvement	Course preparation, small group involvement
	Commitment to my church community, following weekly rhythms locally and as part of wider Order of the Mustard Seed organisation	Commitment to my church community, following weekly rhythms locally and as part of wider Order of the Mustard Seed organisation	Commitment to my church community, following weekly rhythms locally and as part of wider Order of the Mustard Seed organisation	Commitment to my church community, following weekly rhythms locally and as part of wider Order of the Mustard Seed organisation
	Having some personal time of quietness and solitude	Having some personal time of quietness and solitude	Having some personal time of quietness and solitude	Having some personal time of quietness and solitude

	Spring	Summer	Autumn	Winter
Monthly	Writers' group, ongoing projects and seeking new creative outlets	Writers' group, ongoing projects and seeking new creative outlets	Writers' group, ongoing projects and seeking new creative outlets	Writers' group, ongoing projects and seeking new creative outlets
	Commitments as an enthusiastic associate of the Ignatian Spirituality Centre!	Commitments as an enthusiastic associate of the Ignatian Spirituality Centre!	Commitments as an enthusiastic associate of the Ignatian Spirituality Centre!	Commitments as an enthusiastic associate of the Ignatian Spirituality Centre!
	Meeting with friends	Meeting with friends	Meeting with friends	Meeting with friends
Seasonal	Participating in regular local beach cleans	Participating in regular local beach cleans	Participating in regular local beach cleans	Participating in regular local beach cleans
	Time for retreat – both giving and receiving	Time for retreat – both giving and receiving	Time for retreat – both giving and receiving	Time for retreat – both giving and receiving
	Having some longer-term creative goals to explore	Having some longer-term creative goals to explore	Having some longer-term creative goals to explore	Having some longer-term creative goals to explore
Yearly	Observing Lent, and certain other markers in the calendar (Candlemas and solstices are important to me for example)	Attending a particular Christian festival that is a place of deep joy and soul food for our family each summer	Undertaking some formal learning (e.g. recent online course with Glasgow University)	Observing Advent and Candlemas
	Prayerful planning and preparation for annual youth camp/mission	Observing the summer solstice	Observing the autumn equinox	Observing the winter solstice
	Observing the spring equinox			

Faith Habits and How to Form Them

Jill, global conveyor of OMS and author, living in intentional community

	Spring	Summer	Autumn	Winter
Daily	Gratitude practice Silence and solitude *Lectio divina* Rhythms of prayer Daily pages x 3 1.5 hrs writing	Gratitude practice Silence and solitude *Lectio divina* Rhythms of prayer Daily pages x 3 1.5 hrs writing	Gratitude practice Silence and solitude *Lectio divina* Rhythms of prayer Daily pages x 3 1.5 hrs writing	Gratitude practice Silence and solitude *Lectio divina* Rhythms of prayer Daily pages x 3 1.5 hrs writing
Weekly	5 x week community prayer Day of prep and Sabbath (2 days off a week) Coffee date/walk with a friend Reading Receive guests/pilgrims Befriend staff/guests and drop 'gospel seeds' Go to writers' group Read memoirs/historical non-fiction	5 x week community prayer Day of prep and Sabbath (2 days off a week) Coffee date/walk with a friend Reading Receive guests/pilgrims Befriend staff/guests and drop 'gospel seeds' Go to writers' group Read memoirs/historical non-fiction	5 x week community prayer Day of prep and Sabbath (2 days off a week) Coffee date/walk with a friend Reading Receive guests/pilgrims Befriend staff/guests and drop 'gospel seeds' Go to writers' group Read memoirs/historical non-fiction	5 x week community prayer Day of prep and Sabbath (2 days off a week) Coffee date/walk with a friend Reading Receive guests/pilgrims Befriend staff/guests and drop 'gospel seeds' Go to writers' group Read memoirs/historical non-fiction
Monthly	Silent retreat day (bi-monthly) Produce 1 *lectio* 365 and 1 every day with reflection	Silent retreat day (bi-monthly) Produce 1 *lectio* 365 and 1 every day with reflection	Silent retreat day (bi-monthly) Produce 1 *lectio* 365 and 1 every day with reflection	Silent retreat day (bi-monthly) Produce 1 *lectio* 365 and 1 every day with reflection
Seasonal	N/A	N/A	N/A	N/A
Yearly	Take all my annual leave 3–5 day retreat Go to a writers' course/conference	Take all my annual leave 3–5 day retreat Go to a writers' course/conference	Take all my annual leave 3–5 day retreat Go to a writers' course/conference	Take all my annual leave 3–5 day retreat Go to a writers' course/conference

Hopefully these examples show you just how different your rule of life can look, depending on your personality, capacity and preferences. I hope it releases you to really explore, discover and discern how it could look for you.

Creating your own

I'm going to drag your memories back to the beginning of the book where we explored some of the science of habit formation. Remember when I said that it takes at least sixty-six repetitions for a new habit to become familiar and ingrained? That is why I am going to suggest that the very minimum time period you commit trying out your 'rule of life' is three months. This is roughly the length of a season in nature. It isn't so long that it feels like it's never going to end, but it's long enough to form something in us. Then you can do a seasonal review and adjust accordingly.

There is, of course, a caveat to this. You may realise very quickly that something just doesn't work in what you have crafted. These teething problems are completely normal, but once you've adjusted for those initial problems it's time for the 'c' word… commitment. The most common issue that comes up in my one-to-one wellness sessions, when I guide someone through this process, is that they put too much in. Start slowly and kindly, and don't forget to have your 'why' handy as you start crafting your rule. Remember we want our practices to be leading us in the direction we want to go.

What you start with probably won't be where you end up. That's totally OK; you just need to get started. As Rumi said, the way will appear. Crafting a rule of life is much like any endeavour we embark on; we learn along the way.

Here are a few key points to bear in mind:

- Remember that a rule is a living document with plenty of discipline but also realistically flexes with the realities of living in the real world.

- When you are forming your rule of life, ask yourself: 'Am I doing this with both kindness and commitment in mind?'
- This rule of life is a trellis for your life to flourish on, not a list of rules to squeeze the life out of you.
- Understand that it is all grace. There is not a single thing you can do or not do that can increase God's love for you, or God's presence. God's love and presence are already absolute, but you can increase your awareness and experience of those things. Maybe linger in these beautiful words from Psalm 139 as you go:

Where can I go from your Spirit?
>   Where can I flee from your presence?
If I go up to the heavens, you are there;
>   if I make my bed in the depths, you are there.
If I rise on the wings of the dawn,
>   if I settle on the far side of the sea,
even there your hand will guide me,
>   your right hand will hold me fast.
If I say, 'Surely the darkness will hide me
>   and the light become night around me,'
even the darkness will not be dark to you;
>   the night will shine like the day,
>   for darkness is as light to you.

Psalm 139:7–13 NIV

It is such an incredible gift to join in with the divine dance and to be part of co-creation with Christ. You actually get to join with the creator of the entire universe and commune with them, to enter the Trinitarian mystery and join them in bringing the kingdom. It's beyond words.

There is also a simple template for each season, so you can think about how you might want to adapt your rule throughout the year.

But please feel free to use your imagination and creativity here. You can bring in colour, drawing or painting to bring it to life and make it your own.

Once you have drafted your rule, it can be a good idea to discuss it with a soul friend or a spiritual director. They can be more aware of our blind spots at times than we are. It's great for someone to ask you questions such as 'Why do you want to do these certain practices?' and 'Have you overdone it or underdone it?'

Enter the season here e.g. spring
Daily
Weekly
Monthly
Seasonal
Yearly

Final thoughts

> When dragging themselves upstairs to bed, yawning their heads off, Jill said, 'I bet we sleep well tonight'; for it had been a full day. Which shows just how little anyone knows what is going to happen to them next.
> C. S. Lewis, *The Silver Chair*[55]

It has been my absolute privilege to go on this journey with you. Thank you for trusting me to play a small part in your ongoing spiritual formation by allowing me to share some of my thoughts, stories and lessons from the road. I pray it bears much fruit for you, and remember, the best-laid plans and all that... We can put in form and structure to live a life that we hope will lead us to a deeper connection with God, but we have to hold it all lightly. Life is life; don't allow any seasons of discouragement that happen along the way to derail you. It all becomes part of the tapestry.

I'll leave you with one final story about how little control we really have and how God meets us anyway. It was New Year's Eve, 2011, and I had two young kids, Jon was out overnight on a sleep-in at work and all my exhausted little heart wanted was to pray and journal and earnestly read my Bible. I can remember it clear as day – my intentions were so pure. I don't like having my plans interrupted even now, and I've done a huge amount of work on that part of myself, but back then when I had so little time to myself it would feel catastrophic.

Picture the scene: I'm alone on the sofa. I've just got both boys down. I have everything laid around me: books, Bible, journal,

---

[55] C. S. Lewis, *The Silver Chair (The Chronicles of Narnia)* (London: HarperCollins Children's Books, 2001).

blankets and chocolate – I am ready. Then the whole night turns into a nightmare. Both boys got up, one was sick. I was up and down constantly, trying to remain indifferent and love my kids and keep my cool, but I was so sad. Why bother planning anything? I literally never get a minute!

As the clock struck midnight, I was in my bed with both boys cuddling them, journal unopened. In that moment, God broke in and met me where I was. I was flooded with love and purpose and what I now know was a very deep sense of consolation. I was right where I needed to be. No amount of journalling or processing or praying could replace the act of loving my kids and being there for them as only I could on that night. God was teaching me all about the spiritual journey, even though back then I had no language for it. And now here is the book.

It's been hard won. I've been led the really long way round, even though everything in my natural personality wants the quick route and the easy answers. I'm here. I made it. I've not written to please any particular kind of person, and I've probably accidentally offended a few of the people along the way, too. But that's OK. I really hope it blesses you. I've told the truth. I've held nothing back. My life work over the last fifteen years: I release it to you. May it be a tool in releasing you from all that hinders you as you read it.

In John 1, Jesus invites us to 'come and see'. Not just to watch the river or hear the river but dive fully into it and be immersed. God is already fully present. You are already fully loved. Remember, spiritual practices aren't the point; they are just a tool to help us wake up to our deepest reality. The doing, the busyness, the productivity. None of it is the point. The point is love. To be loved and give love the best we can. Your everyday life – that's where the treasure is: the people, the nature, the ordinary glorious stuff and struggles of being human.

At this point in my life, I'm just trying to not miss the goodness of each day, and bring my best self to it.
John Ortberg[56]

The day of my spiritual awakening was the day I saw and knew I saw all things in God and God in all things.
Mechthild of Magdeburg[57]

---

[56] J. M. Comer, *The Ruthless Elimination of Hurry* (London: Hodder and Stoughton, 2019), p. 246, quoting a conversation with John Ortberg.

[57] S. Woodruff, *Meditations with Mechthild of Magdeburg* (Santa Fe, NM: Bear and Co, 1982), p. 42.

Acknowledgements

Thank you to my parents, Neil and Colette, for always believing in me and supporting me. You gave me a childhood filled with love and the freedom to become my own person. I love you both so much. To Ruth and Martin, thank you for welcoming me so wholeheartedly into your family when I married your incredible son.

I'm so blessed to have a life filled with rich friendships, both here in Scotland and down in Cornwall. Special mention goes to Vicky, Louise, Ruth, Anna, Crystal, Kirsten, Tanja, Ness, Bianca, Chantal, Debs and Sara. You are all incredible and I couldn't imagine my life without you!

To Phileena and Amy, I have so much gratitude for how you have guided me through your skilled work as spiritual directors. You both inspire me deeply.

To Lauren Windle and the entire team at SPCK publishing, thank you for your belief in me and this book and for bringing it to life.

To the organisations of 24-7 Prayer and the Order of the Mustard Seed, I have found belonging within your spiritual walls... Thank you.

To East Mountain UK for use of the shepherd's hut and Laure for use of the woodland cabin where the majority of this book was written and wrestled out.

Last but not least, to the five people and one dog who make up my family: Jon, Isaac, Josh, Nate, Soph and Barney, I love you endlessly. No one shows me the heart of God or brings me more sense of joy and home than you.

Further reading

The history

General

The Hawk & The Dove series by Penelope Wilcock
I love these books! Although they are fictional, they are a really good way to feel into the heart and essence of monastic life.

Thomas Merton, *The Wisdom of the Desert: Sayings from the Desert Fathers of the Fourth Century* (New York, NY: New Directions, 1970).
This is a brilliant overview.

Habit formation

Caroline Oakes, *Practice the Pause: Jesus' Contemplative Practice, New Brain Science, and What It Means to Be Fully Human* (Minneapolis, MN: Broadleaf Books, 2023).
This is brilliant if you want to dive deeper into the brain science and Jesus practice.

Thomas Keating, *The Human Condition: Contemplation and Transformation* (New York, NY: Paulist Press, 1999).
A small powerhouse of a book – read it ten times!

Monks, saints and mystics

Claire Gilbert, *I, Julian: The fictional autobiography of Julian of Norwich* (London: Hodder and Stoughton, 2023).
Again, this is fiction, but really captures the essence of Julian; I couldn't put it down.

Ian Morgan Cron, *Chasing Francis: A Pilgrim's Tale* (Grand Rapids, MI: Zondervan, 2013).
Another fictional book; I just love learning about the saints this way!

St John of the Cross, Peter Northcutt, ed., *Dark Night of the Soul: A Modern Translation (The Modern Saints Series — Fresh and Faithful Christian Classics)* (Modern Saints: 2024).
A great modern translation of St John's most famous writing.

Phileena Heuertz, *Pilgrimage of a Soul: Contemplative Spirituality for the Active Life* (Downers Grove, IL: IVP Books, 2010).
Phileena shares her incredible story, including the time she spent in India in the home for the dying where Mother Teresa worked.

Thomas Merton, *The Seven Storey Mountain* (San Diego: Harcourt Brace & Company, 1999).
A wonderful story of the human story and faith journey.

The practices

General

Douglas Kaine McKelvey, *Every Moment Holy, Volume I: New Liturgies for Daily Life* (Nashville, TN: Rabbit Room Press, 2021).
Beautiful prayers for all kinds of occasions. There are other volumes available, too.

The Northumbria Community, *Celtic Daily Prayer: Inspirational prayers & readings from the Northumbria Community* (London: Collins, 2005).
A great daily reading prayer resource; it has more information on the saints, too.

Dennis Linn, Sheila Fabricant Linn, Matthew Linn, *Sleeping with Bread: Holding What Gives You Life* (Mahwah, NJ: Paulist Press, 1995).
A wonderful little book on the prayer of examen.

Ronald Rolheiser, *Domestic Monastery* (London: Darton, Longman & Todd Ltd, 2019).
I only discovered this book recently – it's so brilliant, I wish I had discovered it when my kids were young!

K. J. Ramsey, *The Lord Is My Courage: Stepping Through the Shadows of Fear Toward the Voice of Love* (Grand Rapids, MI: Zondervan, 2022).
A great resource when having a hard time or experiencing/recovering from religious trauma.

Adele Ahlberg Calhoun, *Spiritual Disciplines Handbook: Practices That Transform Us*, revised and expanded ed. (Downers Grove, IL: IVP Books, 2015).
A wonderful resource for learning more about different spiritual practices; great to use on your own or as a group.

A couple of helpful apps for daily prayer
Lectio 365
Pray As You Go fjom

www.ingramcontent.com/pod-product-compliance
Lightning Source LLC
Chambersburg PA
CBHW070150100426
42743CB00013B/2867